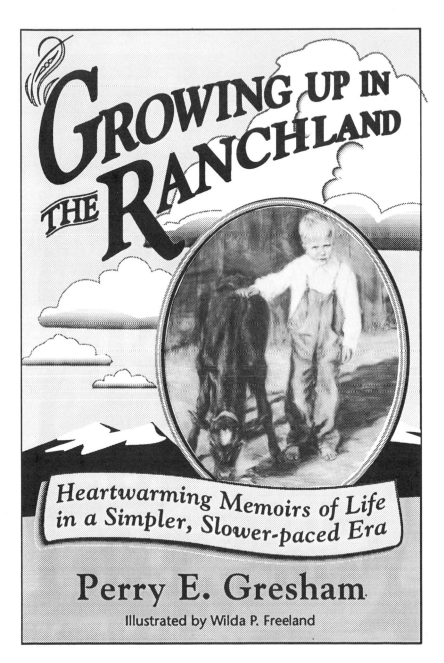

GROWING UP IN THE RANCHLAND

Heartwarming Memoirs of Life in a Simpler, Slower-paced Era

Perry E. Gresham

Illustrated by Wilda P. Freeland

Gaddy Printing Company, P.O. Box 307, Simla, CO 80835

Growing Up in the Ranchland
Heartwarming Memoirs of Life in a Simpler, Slower-paced Era

Copyright © 1994 by Gaddy Printing Company

First printing 1994
Printed in the United States of America

Publisher's Cataloging in Publication
ISBN 0-9619442-2-6

Library of Congress Cataloging-in-Publication Data

Gresham, Perry Epler.
    Growing up in the ranchland : heartwarming memoirs of life in a
simpler, slower-paced era / Perry E. Gresham ; illustrated by Wilda
P. Freeland.
        p.   cm.
    Includes bibliographical references.
    ISBN 0-9619442-2-6 (pbk.) : $12.95
    1. Gresham, Perry Epler--Childhood and youth. 2. Elbert Region
(Colo.)--Biography. 3. Elbert Region (Colo.)--Social life and
customs.   I. Title.
F784.E42G74 1994
978.8'8703'092--dc20
    [B]   93-30417
                                                                 CIP

What they are saying about Perry E. Gresham and his newest book, "Growing Up in the Ranchland."

Perry Gresham is one of the most articulate and interesting people I have known. His achievements, since leaving the ranks of "ranch boy," are remarkable. What he has to say about his beginnings will be instructive and worth the reader's time.

> -- *Robert Allen*
> *Chairman and C.E.O. of A.T.&T.*

I am delighted that *Ranchland News* has seen fit to recognize Dr. Perry Gresham, surely one of this country's distinguished educators, who throughout his career has maintained a sense of view that can only be designated as renaissance in nature. Any person coming in contact with Perry Gresham has been bettered by that experience.

> -- *Gordon Gee*
> *Former President of University of Colorado,*
> *now President of Ohio State University*

Growing Up in the Ranchland is a delight to our hearts. We have known Perry Gresham for a long number of years. We met through our beloved friend and manager, Art Rush, who graduated from Bethany. Art accompanied us to Bethany when Dr. Gresham conferred the Honorary Doctorate of Humanities upon us. Perry Gresham is a remarkable Christian statesman, educator — one who truly lives the Gospel of Jesus Christ. It is an honor to know him. May God bless and speed the travel of this warm account of life in the Ranchland.

> -- *Roy and Dale Rogers*
> *Ranchland world-class celebrities*

Although claiming the entire globe as his home, and rightly so, Perry Gresham nevertheless holds an undeniable fondness for the hardy and spirited people who helped to shape his upbringing in the west. A gifted thinker and a wise man, he is a storyteller second to none. Dr. Gresham, keen of mind and quick of wit, honors the past — his and ours — while never missing a chance to celebrate every new day.

> -- *William Tucker*
> *Chancellor of Texas Christian University*

Dr. Perry E. Gresham has distinguished himself as an academian, corporate director, a platform personality and an author. In this volume he shares experiences that demonstrate endearing values and trust in people that he has gained over a lifetime of associations with time-cherished friends.

> -- *Ivan Gorr*
> *Chairman and C.E.O.,*
> *Cooper Tire and Rubber Co.*

In his youth, Perry Epler Gresham knew the rhythms of the Ranchland, breathed its air and studied its habits. Today, with his facile pen, he writes of the Ranchland with the passion of a native son. Through his graceful style, profound perspectives and imaginative insights, Dr. Gresham makes the land of ranches pulse with life.

> -- *Duane Cummins*
> *President of Bethany College*

Perry Gresham's collection of stories is a home-grown feast. "Growing Up in the Ranchland" is a personal history of a special strength and grace drawn from pioneer times during which life flourished simply from the heart of the American west. As a Colorado Ranchland boy raised on Perry's folksy newspaper column, I knew his writing to possess a humor and close-knit care for the hardy settlers who sought the promise of American life. This is a welcomed volume which continues in the great Gresham tradition.

> -- *George Roche*
> *President of Hillsdale College*

About the Author

"My Uncle Perry"

Dr. Perry Epler Gresham retired as President of Bethany College in 1972 after holding that position for almost twenty years. Continuing in his love of academics, Dr. Gresham spends his retirement lecturing and writing. He has lectured in the United States, Canada, Mexico, England and Scotland. Although his primary field is philosophy, he has also lectured in political economy, religion and gerontology.

Dr. Perry E. Gresham

As a writer, Dr. Gresham has published nine books, including "With Wings as Eagles," which sold more than 26,000 copies. At the age of 85, Dr. Gresham is currently working on his tenth book. He has also seen many of his magazine articles in print. One such article, "Think Twice Before You Disparage Capitalism," was published in "The Freeman" and later reprinted as a pamphlet with a worldwide distribution of 50,000 copies. Dr. Gresham's humor and insight is read weekly by West Virginians in a syndicated column called "The Old Professor."

Prior to his presidency of Bethany College, Dr. Gresham taught at Texas Christian University and lectured at the University of Washington and the University of Michigan. He also served concurrently as a minister in churches near these universities.

Mr. Gresham has practiced his expertise in economics as a corporate director for several companies. These include the Chesapeake and Potomac Telephone Company of West Virginia; Cooper Tire and Rubber Company of Findlay, Ohio; WesBanco Corporation of Wheeling, West Virginia; and the John A. Hartford Foundation of New York City. Although now retired as director of these companies, he still keeps in close contact with them.

Born in Covina, California in 1907, Dr. Gresham moved to a ranch near Elbert, Colorado with his family as a small child. He furthered his education at Texas Christian University, the University of Chicago, Columbia University, and the University of Glasgow.

Today Dr. Gresham and his wife, Aleece, divide their time between their home in Bethany, West Virginia, and their second home in Bermuda Village at Advance, North Carolina. Dr. Gresham also keeps an office at Bethany College.

by Gale Gresham, Free lance writer

Acknowledgments

This little book would not have been possible had it not been for the help of my publisher, Monty Gaddy, the typing and retyping of the manuscript by my colleague, Karen Atkinson, the careful reading and suggestions of my academic colleague, Dr. Pauline Nelson, and the beautiful, artistic drawings of my distinguished artist and friend, Wilda Freeland.

I am also grateful to my wife, Aleece Gresham, who read each of these documents, and to my sister, Bernice Roberts of Colorado Springs, and my brother, Harvey Gresham of Carthage, Missouri, who have supplied me with much of the data.

About the illustrator

Wilda P. Freeland is a portrait painter who has won national and international awards for the beauty and excellence of her work. She contributed the illustrations for this volume, as well as the painting which is reproduced on the cover.

Her prize winning portrait, "Hilary," which was published in "The Illustrator," an international magazine, won fame for her unusual talent.

She paints landscapes and still life as well. She was, for seventeen years, fashion illustrator for the Stone and Thomas department stores of West Virginia. She has the rare gift of breathing life and a new dimension into a flat canvas.

Among her many portraitures are Dr. Gresham, Courtney Burton, Tony Gentile, Mr. and Mrs. Ernest Discher and Dorothy Stephens Moore.

Her studio is at Wellsburg, West Virginia.

Table of Contents

She lived through her 90th birthday with the same equanimity that that she had maintained through two major wars and the Great Depression.

My father caught me once in a little white lie. His explanation of the result of lying was punishment enough.

It was the land of the buffalo and the plains Indians... Into this land came the hunters, who were followed by the ranchers.

I have been more lonely in New York, London, Paris, Athens, or in Beijing or Bombay, than I ever felt on that ranch, even though the nearest ranch house was a quarter mile away.

At first, many ranch homes lacked bathrooms with indoor plumbing, even though ours had the room and the tub. The path outdoors was the way of life then.

Those brave pioneer men soon opened some tracks through the snow into the town of Elbert. Elsner's store and Harper's store were very glad to have some trade once more. They were soon sold out of overshoes.

At last my turn came, and I walked proudly that quarter of a mile where a whole new world came into view. My teacher, for there was only one for all classes through grade eight, was more than a teacher to me; she seemed more like some goddess who could bring treasures of knowledge and discovery.

Chapter 8
Abandoned 22
When I came out, the family was gone. At first I did not panic, but assumed they would return for me. As time whent on, I began to worry. I stood there on the corner looking in all directions, but there was no sign of our car or the Cantrell car. I began to cry.

Chapter 9
Jakey 25
I was too small for a saddle pony. To my delight, my father bought me a donkey! My size and weight suited the donkey to a tee. I rode him around wherever he wanted to go.

Chapter 10
Pets...27
Her little girl, Betty Jo, was so taken with the little pigs that she wanted to take one into the house. When Dad objected, she asked, "Why?" Dad said, "Because it is not done in the best of families." She countered, "But Uncle George, we are not the best of families!"

Chapter 11
What We Heard and Read 30
The phonograph came early to the Ranchland. Every home seemed to have a "Victrola." Ours was a stand-up model with a side crank.

Chapter 12
Fairs..32
Going to the fairs was one of the joys of my Ranchland youth. We had a fine nearby fair in Elbert, and we traveled to Calhan and to Castle Rock.

Chapter 13
Recreation..34
One Sunday afternoon, a violent rainstorm came up and a team that had come from Denver to play against Elbert was stranded in the mud. We put them up at our house and let them sleep in the clean hay of our barn loft. My mother, bless her, fed the whole lot.

Chapter 21
Discourse of the Early Ranchland 55

The Ranchland of my youth had some colorful expressions which I have heard but seldom, if at all, since those days.

Chapter 22
Twilight Memories 58

Growing up in the Ranchland was a great privilege, and I would not trade that beginning for marble halls and storied palaces!

Chapter 23
Pranksters 61

The teenage boys were out for pranks. They would play visiting goblins to the entire neighborhood. Standard pranks consisted of upsetting the outhouses.

Chapter 24
Winter 63

My saddle horse seemed to love the cold weather as much as I did. I carried a pocket full of oats to reward him when he came at my call.

Chapter 25
Community 65

Our closest neighbor lost his comfortable ranch house in a fire... Food, lodging and clothing were supplied by the neighbors until arrangements were made and the building replaced.

Chapter 26
The Charivari 67

After the wedding, which was held either in the home of the bride or at a church, the young friends would prepare some outlandish sounds to annoy the young people on their wedding night.

Chapter 27
Throwaways 69

"Every gambler knows the secret of survival is knowing what to throw away and knowing what to keep." My life would have been richer and better if I could have known and practiced that wise maxim.

Chapter 34

I was old enough to wonder why my older friends had to die on the battlefields of France. I sang the songs with gusto and belief, but I have never ceased to wonder why we cannot find some better way.

Chapter 35

The Great Western Stock Show in Denver was a ranch boy's dream come true... we drove into Elbert and caught the train.

Chapter 36

My father asked Mr. Peterson if his fine stallion could breed one of the Gresham mares... The eagerness of the stallion got out of hand and the event occurred right there in the center of town. Women hurried by, looking the other way.

Chapter 37

I placed a can of beans in the campfire to get it warm before I opened it. The can exploded and spattered my lady friend with baked beans! I was both embarrassed and ridiculed.

Chapter 38

I can still see the distinguished men of the Ranchland with watch fobs and stickpins as they gathered to discuss the weather and new breeds of cattle.

Chapter 39

I had a team run away when I was raking hay. The bumpy ride knocked me off the seat and down to where the tines were about to roll me over and over.

Chapter 40

When I grew a little older I asked my father how a porcupine could possibly make love. He said, "Very carefully!"

When I shifted down into low I brought the gear into play too abruptly and it snapped the drive shaft. Not only was the power gone, but also the brakes! I was going backward down a steep mountain.

My mother taught me that if a person could afford two loaves of bread, he should buy one loaf and a lotus blossom.

My first experience was with a box Brownie. It was very nearly foolproof and it took fairly good pictures. I cherished it as if it were a treasure from some mystic land.

Dr. Denny covered a range of 20 miles with a team and buggy to keep us well and alive as long as possible.

I became familiar with many varieties of cars by visiting the showrooms; but of most interest to me were the displays of saddlery at Herman Henry Heiser's shop on Larimer Street.

He stepped out of the large black Buick and told me he had come to personally invite me to be a student at his college. I told him that I was a high school drop-out.

When I was living at home on the ranch, I had developed something of the art of business. I knew, almost instinctively, that the art consisted of buying low and selling high.

Chapter 48
Courtship and Marriage 122

Elsie's parents and their friends were skeptical about Elsie's marriage to a young ranch lad who had not yet found gainful employment beyond the small salary paid to him by the tiny church.

Chapter 49
The Lure of Texas 124

The new pastor, a solid Texan, took me under his wing at once and arranged for Elsie and me to move to Texas, where I could study at Texas Christian University.

Chapter 50
The Lure of the Ranchland 126

This was my home, and I returned to it as naturally as the salmon brave the steep rocks of the Columbia River to spawn.

Chapter 51
Ranchland Revisited................................128

We pulled into Elbert to find it smaller than when I moved away... many of my familiar haunts had been swept away in the flood of 1936.

Chapter 52
The Groves of Academe 131

I loved learning and to this day I am still a student. I started teaching at 24, and it has been my life.

CHAPTER 1

Tribute to a Pioneer Woman

On a pleasant July day in Colorado, I joined my family in a tribute to a pioneer woman named Mary Elizabeth Epler Gresham. We drove from the base of Pikes Peak to the little village of Elbert, located somewhat east of the axis between Denver and Colorado Springs. A memorial service in the white frame church recounted the triumphs of a life that began in 1876, when buffalo roamed the plateau and Indians came to barter.

Mary Epler lost her mother when she was a very little girl, but the stalwart father, Daniel Epler, soon found a widow named Abigail Martin, who proved to be a splendid mother for little Mary and her siblings. The little girl grew to womanhood surrounded by love mixed with hard work. Ranch life then was largely won from the somewhat reluctant land. Yet she found time to paint and play the piano. She was pretty — almost beautiful. A strong young man named

George Gresham came west to work on the Epler ranch. He had come from southern Missouri, across Kansas, in a buckboard. They fell in love and were married in that high country decorated with pine trees. The century of speed and steel, transportation and communication, had not yet been born. They were pioneers together, tilling their land, growing their livestock and raising their babies.

Mary Gresham loved birds and little animals. Her turkeys and chicks were the pride of the Divide country. She loved flowers and vegetables; her garden yielded golden chrysanthemums and pumpkins, as well as green cucumbers, cabbages and warty squash. She gathered chokecherries and turned them into the most delectable jelly. She was a hostess of note in the countryside. Neighbors and family came from miles around to share her fried chicken, sweet corn, potato soup, homemade ice cream and black raspberry dumplings.

Her ranch house was clean and tidy, even though her outdoor chores were numerous and complicated. Her four children grew to able manhood and womanhood with inner confidence and security, and they all had enough culture and education to take their places in several communities with stature and dignity. They felt no sense of privation for living far from the urban centers that were, even then, beginning to swallow the countryside.

She knew how to look in the eye of an angry bull or to help a young mare with the birth of her first foal. She could drive a team when occasion required. But she always looked to George Gresham for leadership. When he died, at 87, she lived on lonely, but she met the exigencies of those subsequent years with poise and courage. Children, grandchildren, great-grandchildren and neighbors swarmed around her rocking chair, which then was located in her daughter's Colorado Springs house. She lived through her 90th birthday with the same equanimity that she had maintained through two major wars and the Great Depression. She did not whine or lose command of herself when age brought silent darkness, as her sight and hearing departed. She had acquired something of the patience and endurance of the mountains she loved.

She died at home, not caring for hospitals and the institutional practices that often belong to them. Her strong old heart failed her, and she went to her last sleep. Her son offered a prayer of gratitude for her life, and praise for the good Lord whose wisdom sets boundaries for human existence. She was buried beside her late husband, her father and her father's father in the charming Elbert Cemetery, which looks out toward Cretaceous rocks, pine trees and everlasting hills.

As I said goodbye to my family and drove off toward Denver, I could only think that I would have loved and honored this woman, even if she had not been my mother.

CHAPTER 2

Parents

I need none of the usual sentimental gush to describe my mother. I learned trust at her breast, caring on her knee and endurance by her example. She carried me through the life-threatening illness of typhoid fever when I was very young.

She taught me to care about animals. The ranchers' attitude toward livestock was not enough. I became aware that branding and castrating young animals gave them terrible pain. She cared about saddle sores on my pony and collar sores on work horses. She did not know of the Schweitzer "reverence for life" philosophy but had feelings for all creatures. Her regard for the feelings of rats and snakes, however, did not dissuade her from dispatching them.

She gave me vision. When I had played hard and long, then came into the house at twilight, she would be playing "Over The Waves" on the piano. I wondered what was beyond the waves, and I have spent more than eighty years trying to find out. "Over The Hills And Far Away" was one of her favorite quotations. The vision of my life goes out beyond the horizon. Mystery and wonder have carried me into philosophy and on toward the great beyond.

I left home when I was but sixteen, but on return visits I always admired my mother as about the most beautiful woman in the Ranchland. She had taught me self-reliance without dominating me, and had instilled in me the virtues of work, honesty and frugality. She did not spoil me, but she surrounded me with love so that I did not feel deprived. She expected me to live up to her standards, and she knew how to reprove me with a glance. I do not remember a spanking of any kind for any thing. Her beauty was not studied, nor applied. She was a well dressed ranch woman who needed no beauty parlor.

She was bright enough, but not what one would call an intellectual. She was more heart than head. Convictions? She had them and clung to them. She listened politely to differing opinions, but her mind was closed to them. She had some fears: lightning and hail storms were among them. She was always afraid of depletion of the water supply.

Among her strongest loves, beyond that of her family, were those Colorado mountains and her ranch home. Her years in California were miserable. She preferred the precarious Ranchland, with its dry weather, exposure to hail, furious blizzards and isolation, to all the values of a warm climate and an urban comfort. She belonged to the earth and the sky.

Her father, Daniel Epler, was a retired veteran of the Union Army. He had marched with Sherman and was wounded. He carried a musket ball for the rest of his life. Yet he was a successful rancher with the brand "DE." He, along with his brothers, had gone west at the close of the war. They were Pennsylvania Dutch and wore the Biblical names of Isaac, Simeon and Jacob. Their sister, Mary, stayed in Illinois. It was to the Epler Ranch, hard by Running Creek, that my father came seeking employment. He was hired. He proved himself and married the rancher's daughter.

George Gresham was the son of Elijah, who, with his brother, Nathan, was a Texas Ranger. Elijah moved about, but he was in Carthage, Missouri, when my father was born. Both parents died when Dad was very young.

When Dad was old enough, he acquired a team and buckboard and headed west. He wound up on the Epler ranch where he met and married my mother. The year was 1899.

Through the haze of memory, I see my father as very kind, considerate, honest and trustworthy. He was very bright. When a kidney disease struck him in mid-life he did not surrender. The medicos did what they could, but he was in danger. He saw an advertisement for the Palmer School of Chiropractic. He had been helped by manipulation of muscles and adjustment of bones on previous occasions, so he drove to Denver, where the school was located, and applied for admission as a student.

The dean asked for his academic background. He was unlettered, even unschooled with but minor exceptions. The dean pointed out the impossibility of his entering and doing the work. He would be pitted against young college graduates. He told the dean that he wanted a chance. The dean gave him permission to enroll in chemistry; if he made the grade he would be considered. He not only passed, but he led the class!

He had no intention of practicing. All he wanted was a means of recovery. He became an expert in nutrition and had the advantage of health procedures from his teachers and fellow students. He finished the course, received his degree and impressed the family with his cap and gown! With the help of some prostatic surgery later, he lived to the ripe age of 87. His only practice was with his family and a few neighbors.

My boyhood was not lived in wealth, but Dad was prosperous. He was frugal without being stingy. He was a community leader. He was Clerk of the Session at the Presbyterian Church and twice delegate to the National General Assembly. He was state president of the Grange, and state president of the Odd Fellows Lodge. He was a wheel in the local Republican Party.

He was very quick at mental arithmetic. His management of his ranch, and previously of two grocery stores, made good use of his math. He helped me with my problems when I was learning in the little school. He was versatile. He read widely and was eloquent in public address. He had a strong body and could do most anything that ranch life required.

He was kind, gentle and caring with me. I was at home longer than my siblings and thereby found considerable advantage. We were often in Denver, where I once saw George Arliss on the stage and, on another occasion, heard Caruso sing "Girl Of The Golden West." He taught me geography and self-reliance as we drove to California and to Carmel, Illinois.

I was proud of him and loved him. I felt no impulse to rebel as most ranch boys did. He taught me to work hard. I was a full ranch hand at fourteen.

He caught me once in a little lie. His explanation of the result of lying was punishment enough. The little lie involved my new pocket knife. I had seen Dad make a knife out of a nail by heating it and hammering it out on the anvil. I tried that with my new knife with disastrous results. When he asked me what had happened, I told him I had dropped it on the anvil! That was about as incredible as it could be!

When Elsie and I were married, my parents presented us with a new Ford car. The gift came not with opulence, but from love. My parents, my sister Bernice, my brothers Frank and Harvey were a perfect family for my youth. They all looked after me, and I loved it.

CHAPTER 3

Ranchland

"Ranchland" is just the right name for the high plateau that stretches eastward from the Rocky Mountain foothills. The land is high; most of it well over 6,000 feet. Along an almost imperceptible ridge, the rainwater divides, with some of it running northward toward the Platte River and some of it running southward toward the Arkansas; hence, it is called "The Divide Country." It was the land of the buffalo and the plains Indians, who lived by hunting, first with bow and arrow, then with guns, for which they traded their furs and hides. Into this land came the hunters, who were followed by the ranchers. Each rancher had his own brand. The range was wide and grassy; the cattle thrived.

The pioneers were taking up land and building homes when my grandfather, Daniel Epler, arrived. He "homesteaded" on Running Creek and ran cattle on the range. His brand was

"DE." Several of his brothers had come west with him. They bore the Biblical names Isaac, Jacob and Simeon. My mother, Mary Epler, was native to the Ranchland, but life there was not easy. When she was 22 years old, George Gresham, from Carthage, Missouri, found employment on the Epler ranch and won the heart and hand of Mary Epler.

This newly married couple and some of the Eplers moved westward to California. There, in a town named Covina hard by the San Dimas Wash, in a bungalow located in an orange grove, I was born. My mother longed for the open land, the wide sky and the view of Pikes Peak. The Ranchland was her home, and she wished to return. In strong feminine fashion, she persisted and finally had her way. I was only four years old when we returned to Colorado. The cattle, the chickens, a cat and a dog in that spacious new home were as dear to me as they were to my mother. The year was 1912.

The old house on the land my father had repossessed was aged and infirm; you might say it was rickety. Jens Olkjer was employed to build a new house patterned after the California house in which I was born. My eyes were as wide as the new windows when the home arose from the cement foundation. To me it was a mansion, but when I see it now it seems to be a modest, but commodious, bungalow. That was the Ranchland home of my childhood, my boyhood and my youth.

I was a generation or two away from the open range where cowboys had their roundup and branding parties. My family and our neighbors had taken to farming, as well as breeding cattle and other livestock. I knew the plow, the drill, the cultivator and the binder, as well as the rope, the saddle and those wonderful horses.

Our ranch was about four miles west of the town. There were dirt roads and few cars. Travel was by spring wagon on weekdays and by buggy on Sundays. People in a hurry used saddle horses. Produce and anything heavy was by wagon.

The Colorado and Southern Railroad, a considerable factor in the settlement and development of the Divide Country, came through Elbert. From time to time, our family would take the train to Denver. I loved it, but my best fun came when we drove to Colorado Springs in a surrey. When a shower came up, we could roll down the side curtains. Sometimes we could spend the night in the ranch house of my Uncle Charley, who lived at Eastonville. He had a large barn, big enough to accommodate 40 cattle. His hayloft seemed as large as the mountains.

Sixty-five years have rolled by since I packed my clothes into the trunk of my Buick roadster and headed down the dirt road toward Denver. I have returned on several occasions, but only to visit. My Ranchland boyhood seems far away and long ago. My memories, however, are vivid and lasting.

CHAPTER 4

Lonely in the Ranchland? Never!

Loneliness never occurred to me when I was a small child in the Ranchland. With my older brothers and my sister at school and my father at work in some distant field, I was alone with my very busy mother. Not once do I remember a moment when I felt lonely. I have been more lonely in New York, London, Paris, Athens, or in Beijing or Bombay, than I ever felt on that ranch, even though the nearest ranch house was a quarter mile away, and the next one was a full mile away. There was my dog to play with and the most wonderful rocks, where I pretended I had my own house with many rooms. Small pieces of lovely quartz were the people, and bits of broken glass were the dishes.

On occasion my mother would prepare a little lunch for me, and I would go down to the rocks where I could watch the cottontails, the mountain bluebirds, the wild geese as they flew southward. I listened to the sound of the sickle

as my father cut hay in a nearby field. No
sandwich ever tasted better than those prepared
by my mother. My dessert was a small slice of
cantaloupe which was worth waiting for. My
mother's arms were warm and tender when I
came home. Ranchland life was beautiful!

I was always waiting for my siblings when
they returned from school. Bernice would give me
some lessons in writing and reading, even though
I was only five. I learned to snip all sorts of
objects from a piece of paper using the blunter
scissors she provided. I could make a horse, a
cow, a dog, a house, and almost any object by
folding the paper and forming the two sides at
once. When the paper was unfolded, there was an
object to admire!

While my brothers helped my father in the
fields, my sister helped my mother in preparing
supper. There were peas to shell, beans to snap
and potatoes to peel. As the kitchen range was
stoked for cooking, the most heavenly aroma came
from the house. I shall never forget the redolence
of fried potatoes and onions, and that homemade
soup was fit for the gods!

After supper we would sometimes play
caroms or dominos. Occasionally we played
parlor games, such as hide-and-seek, or ring
around the roses. I was fascinated with the
pictures on playing cards. The kings, queens and
jacks sent my young imagination soaring. My
family included me in simple card games even
before I was of school age. That was long ago; I
still remember Ranchland evenings.

CHAPTER 5

Homes on the Range

Our new house was built in 1913 by a genius named Jens Olkjer. In fact, most of the Ranchland houses in our area were his expert handiwork. He was neither architect nor contractor; he was both of these and more. He was carpenter, engineer, bricklayer, cement expert, and whatever else was required in the building of a house. He was the master builder of the schoolhouse where I learned the basics that have sustained me through a long and successful academic career. I shall never forget the magic of how this man built our house; it was as if a musician played an entire concert by ear. He just knew what to do and did it. Our house, our barn and our schoolhouse still stand.

I have traveled a bit around the Ranchland, and everywhere I have seen Jens Olkjer's houses. We always felt secure and comfortable in an Olkjer house. His descendants still live in the Elbert area. The Olkjer houses do not look alike; some are large, some small, some one-story and some multi-story, but they are all sturdy and worthy of survival. There was not much status-symbol competition among the early ranchers. They were a practical lot and eager to have shelter and reasonable comfort. At first, they mostly lacked bathrooms with indoor plumbing, even though ours had the room and the tub. The path outdoors was the way of life then.

Six of us lived in that house; my parents, George and Mary Gresham, and my three siblings: Harvey, who was born in 1901, Frank, who was born in 1903 and who died on a bitter cold day in late 1990, and Bernice, who was born in 1905.

We were happy there. The sound of our laughter still lingers in my memory. That home west of Elbert is the only childhood home I can clearly remember. Cold water from the adjacent well, the redolence of frying potatoes and onions, the lovely aroma of cinnamon rolls coming out of the oven, the warm water from the range reservoir on a cold day — these memories are forever.

We were not wealthy, nor were we poor. I suppose most people of that time would call us "well-to-do." When a neighbor came to my father to borrow some money, I saw Dad take a checkbook from his pocket and write a check for $10,000. Those Ranchland pioneers were a provident lot and had retained the virtue of thrift and industry as well as the most cherished virtue of honesty. Nobody dared violate a handshake; the neighborhood would have shunned him.

That was a great place for us to mature. God bless the Ranchland!

CHAPTER 6

The Big Snow

Whittier's *Snowbound* begins, "The sun that brief December day rose cheerless over hills of gray." So it was in the Ranchland on December 7, 1913. I was just about to turn six years old. We were in our new house where we were warm and cozy. The snow came down so relentlessly that vision was impaired, if not obscured. Harvey, Frank and Bernice were in school a quarter of a mile away; I was too young. Come afternoon, with the snow still cascading down, my father saddled a horse and rode to the schoolhouse. He knew that his pony knew the way home without being able to see the road.

Following the homebound horse were my siblings and the Brazleton children. The snow continued for three days. Four feet of snow on the level and drifts twelve feet high were heard of in that dry country. The Ranchland turned to white and stayed that way until March! Fortunately, my mother always had a storehouse of food. Dad and the older boys tunneled through a drift to attend the livestock in the barn. The snow was so deep that when I looked out the upstairs window, I saw only snow! I loved every minute of it. No more thoughts of California poppies. Frank made a sort of toboggan out of barrel staves and slid down from the high window. He let me ride along when he was sure it was safe.

Thank God for those old barrels! Dad and the older boys made snowshoes so that we could move from one place to another. We made caves, but Dad put a stop to that. He knew the danger of a cave-in. Soon Mr. Brazleton came to reclaim his children, but that was after the snow had ceased. Four horses tandem were required to pull the wagon through those heavy drifts. Those brave pioneer men soon opened some tracks through the snow into the town of Elbert. Elsner's store and Harper's store were very glad to have some trade once more. They were soon sold out of overshoes.

I was sorry when March winds turned the white hills into sepia. I had made snowmen, thrown snowballs, snowshoed and played around the ranch house. Such a snow as that one has not come again.

Moisture was plentiful all over the Ranchland. Tall green grass came for pasture, and all crops were abundant. Debate still goes on among the old-timers as to how deep the snow was on the level. Four feet is my best word.

CHAPTER 7

School Days

Those wise and provident pioneers had arranged for school lands to be set aside. When the land was sold off, there was money to build a schoolhouse. Ours was named Lincoln School and was a fine little frame structure built by that amazing Jens Olkjer.

I could hardly wait until I was six years old and could start to school. My sister, Bernice, was a natural teacher, and by the time I could attend classes she had already taught me to read and write. My two older brothers and my sister were enrolled in school, and I waited for them to return after four o'clock. They always had fascinating stories of what they had learned that day. At last my turn came, and I walked proudly that quarter of a mile where a whole new world came into view. My teacher, for there was only one for all classes through grade eight, was more than a teacher to me; she seemed more like some goddess who could bring treasures of knowledge and discovery. The joy of learning, which began there, has been the dominant melody of my long life.

A one-room schoolhouse has some advantages unknown to our present system of separate grades and many teachers. I learned as much from the recitation of the more advanced classes as I did from my own. I had as fair a knowledge of eighth grade geography and history when I was only in the lower grades as I had when I had finished the final grade. I always worked about six weeks ahead of the assignments. I devoured every book in our modest school library. I loved the books about Holland and Switzerland, and daydreamed about going there some day. I could not imagine that 75 years later my visits to Lucerne and Amsterdam would be as commonplace as our visits to Colorado Springs or Denver were then.

When I close my eyes I can see again the little green schoolhouse where I began my academic pilgrimage. It still stands, and I love it!

CHAPTER 8

Abandoned

The automobile transformed the Ranchland. While we had often driven a horse-drawn rig to Colorado Springs, we drove often in our new gas buggies. The Greshams and the Cantrells set forth one morning for what we called "The Springs," that exciting city located at the foot of Pikes Peak. It was about 35 miles from our ranch.

I was just out of the second grade. It was an exciting event for all of us, but especially for me. It changed my life, and I shall tell you why. Our families spent the day shopping. We enjoyed a picnic in Palmer Park. It was a great experience, but then it happened.

As we made ready to leave Colorado Springs for home, I went into the corner drug store to buy some family-authorized object with the money I had saved. We were to meet at that corner. When I came out, the family was gone. At first I did not panic, but assumed they would return for me. As time went on, I began to worry. I stood on the corner looking in all directions, but there was no sign of our car or the Cantrell car. I began to cry. People noticed and consoled me with the thought that my family would soon miss me and return.

Finally, while driving along, my mother began to wonder if I was really in the Cantrell car as she had supposed. Dad tooted Tom Cantrell to a halt and, sure enough, I was the missing member of the party. They wheeled about in a hurry. They were already several miles out of town.

Meanwhile, time moved slowly for me. I began to think about what would happen to me if they did not return before dark. I cried. I watched with longing and disappointed eyes. I prayed and felt completely lost and abandoned. People, in pity, offered to take me to their homes, but I was afraid to leave the spot on which we were to gather for departure. The big clock on the corner kept ticking away, and the quarter hour chimes kept sounding.

Tom Cantrell looked like salvation personified when he roared up to the curb, jumped out and gathered me in his powerful arms. He was more of a daredevil driver than my father, but Dad was there in another minute. The relief was beyond description. I was overwhelmed with joy.

Now I am in my middle eighties, and I still have nightmares about being forgotten and alone in a strange city. That traumatic experience of a small boy has left a psychological scar. I have always been afraid I would be left behind.

It has been my good fortune, throughout my

long life, to be with people who are careful not to leave me in predicaments where I feel abandoned. I have tended to be punctual, for the penalty of that early Ranchland experience is too poignant to ignore.

CHAPTER 9

Jakey

The Shetland pony was not very popular in our little world. A Shetland was not utilitarian — it was too citified. When a child was old enough to manage a pony, the ranch parent thought of a small saddle horse that could carry the child to such useful enterprises as fetching the milk cows or running errands for the family. I was too small for such a saddle pony, and to my delight, my father bought me a donkey!

This was no gray and fuzzy little beast with enormous ears; this was a good-sized black beast with a first-rate mind and strong opinions. I was afraid to mount him, and Dad offered to show me how to ride the new household critter. He mounted bareback. The ass bucked twice as he took off at high speed, then planted his feet firmly in the Colorado clay. Dad slid over his head and landed on <u>his</u> donkey.

We named my donkey Jakey. His breed had

no withers, which made it easy for Jakey to buck twice, make a fast start and plant his feet.

My size and weight suited the donkey to a tee. I rode him around wherever he wanted to go. I had a new saddle and blanket, but also a new harness and a snappy little cart. I cut quite a figure when I took a solo ride with Jakey accoutered in brass-knobbed hames and shiny bridle rosettes. I won fame and a prize at the Elbert County Fair when Lincoln School permitted me to drive in back of their big hayrack which had been decorated with green and white crepe paper; the colors of Lincoln School. As I, with the help of Jack Brazleton, drove Jakey behind the float, he amused himself by eating the paper flowers from the float! The spokes of my cart were laced with red, white and blue. We were more photographed than the prize big float.

One day when my cousin, Lela Epler, came to visit, we saddled Jakey and rode down the piney bluff of the Epler Ranch. We enjoyed a happy lunch while Jakey ate the oats we provided. As we started home, he acted tired. One of us walked, then both of us walked; finally we carried the saddle up the slope while Jakey complained of the steep climb. He was a clever beast!

Later, as I grew older, I had many saddle horses to ride, and one to own. None was as dear to me as that strong-willed ass from the primitive Asian plateaus. Jakey is a Ranchland legend.

CHAPTER 10

Pets

Every ranch house had dogs, and our house was no exception, but we had only one at a time. Among those I most remember was a black curly critter of mixed parentage which we called "Colonel." He was my staunch companion. I had some difficulty explaining to him that he should not follow me to school. He always made my homecoming a great occasion; we romped and chased each other until I gave up. That dog had boundless energy. He nipped at the heels of one of the horses and, shortly thereafter, went to dog heaven.

We had a larger dog of mongrel lineage named "Major." He was a tannish-brown dog that was always in some kind of health difficulty. He was a brave beast and loyal to a fault. He sickened and died, but it came gradually and we were not so shocked and grieved.

My best pal was a small goat. I have

noticed that almost all horse farms have a goat around to calm the horses. We had this goat because he was as cute as he was destructive. He loved to climb to the very top of anything around. He jumped up on the very top of any car. His sharp hooves were damaging to the finish, and disastrous to a ragtop. He would eat almost anything, such as the sleeve of my coat. I cannot remember why I was so charmed by the little rascal, but I do remember I cried most of the night when one of our horses placed a well aimed hoof to end the annoyance.

We had plenty of cats. I felt childish outrage when I found that tomcats killed the little kittens. I was always enthralled when I saw a mother carry the young in her mouth. I was also amazed at the mother's ability to hide the place of her family beginnings. Cats were so fecund that they were a problem; they were too much of a problem to neuter, and too reproductive to control. We did not approve of the drowning method; we always gave them to some willing neighbor. I remember a famous West Virginia bird artist named Ray Harm saying that he lived so far back in the mountains that they had to keep their own tomcat. We always had too many toms around.

Most ranchers were too utilitarian for exotic pets, although I knew of one person who had a pet monkey. We always thought he should get an organ to grind, or else get rid of the funny creature. Our favorite pets, other than those I have mentioned, were lambs, calves, colts and piglets. Little chickens and turkeys were also much cherished.

When my cousin Hazel Baldwin came to visit, her little girl, Betty Jo, was so taken with the little pigs that she wanted to take one into the house. When Dad objected, she asked, "Why?"

Dad said, "Because it is not done in the best of families".

She countered, "But Uncle George, we are not the best of families!"

CHAPTER 11

What We Heard and Read

The phonograph came early to the Ranchland. Every home seemed to have a "Victrola." Some had the big horn-type, as pictured in the advertisements always with the spotted dog and the cornucopia projector with the words, "His master's voice." Ours was a stand-up model with a side crank. The records were of a varied order, but some of quality. I learned many of the songs from "The Student Prince" and bits from "Aida" and from "Il Trovatore." We had bits of humor, such as "Uncle Josh" and "The Preacher and the Bear." From "Uncle Josh," I remember his having slipped on a banana peel and fallen on his derriere. His friend said, "I don't think much of a person who would throw a banana peel on the sidewalk." Uncle Josh responded, "I think less of the banana peel that would throw a person on the sidewalk!" Well, all right, it seemed funny to me then.

Then came the radio. The game was to see what faraway stations could be reached and identified even though the reception was poor. I remember my pride at having heard KDKA in Pittsburgh. Creative boys were building their own sets. Some of them were rather impressive. I tried a little, but with small success. We did get up-to-the-minute news from KOA in Denver. We also heard fine music and fascinating humor from "Amos 'n' Andy." Live broadcasts of big events gave local color. We were able to participate in the visits of presidents, and in notable sporting events. The air waves promoted the National Western Stock Show and similar occasions of interest to ranch boys.

Television came too late; I had left my ranch home for the trials and challenges of urban and academic life by the time the tube took over. We were long on papers, however, and I still remember the headlines about the war as they appeared in *The Denver Post*. While still a boy, I became aware of the campaign which carried Woodrow Wilson to his victory over Hughes. I loved the funny papers with "Foxy Granpa," "Old Doc Yak," "The Katzenjammer Kids" and "Buster Brown." When I was older, I read the want ad section to locate things I wished to buy.

I always had some money; I saved it as if I were a miser, but I acquired it by my father's gift of two heifer calves, which became cows and gave me the increase. As I grew older, I worked for the neighbors in slack times and earned a little. For certain kinds of work my father paid me money. I knew, however, that it was I who owed him.

CHAPTER 12

Fairs

Going to the fair was one of the joys of my Ranchland youth. We had a fine nearby fair in Elbert, and we traveled to Calhan and to Castle Rock. We often attended the "Pikes Peak or Bust" Fair in Colorado Springs. My love for the fairs centered mainly on the exhibits, in which I often competed, and frequently won some minor honors for garden produce or school art. The cotton candy caught my eye but once; then I avoided it like the plague. The horse racing was very exciting. Some of the participants did not like the calls and managed to get into some Ranchland fights.

The rodeos were best of all. I grew up with the blood of the old west and the cowboy heritage. I started swinging a rope when I was still a small boy and kept at it until I left the ranch in my later teens. I roped fence posts for practice and then went for my pet calves. They put up with me, but they were not delighted with my roping. When I was older, I rode my saddle horse down into the timber, cut a Christmas tree and snaked it home through the snow by means of my lariat.

I learned to ride bucking horses fairly well, got thrown once, and pulled leather often. I loved to watch the professionals ride the Brahma bulls. The clown seemed to be fearless and foolhardy. At one of the fairs — I forget which one — someone told me the fair director was going to enlist some Indians to put on a dance. With limited funds, they found some braves from the reservation who had no experience in show business. They asked the bucks to dance dressed in chaps. The Indians did not realize the chaps have no seat in them, so they danced with just their hot-weather attire under the chaps. The dance displayed the Indians' underwear to the amusement of some of the ruder members of the community.

That Calhan fair brought people from all over the Ranchland. It was an opportunity to see old friends and compare notes on the dry weather. Ranchers were always keen on improving their herds. They occasionally bought some prize bulls while attending the friendly gathering.

The dirt roads were a problem. If a fierce rain came, some roads became impassable. The experienced men always had chains when needed in order to pull the steepest hills. The hard work of fair attendance was equal to the hard work they all knew at home. As a little boy, I had the fun without the work!

CHAPTER 13

Recreation

The air at our home was clear and pure. Stars were so bright that one could almost reach up and touch them. When morning came, the first rays of the sun would be reflected from the snowy summit of Pikes Peak. The mountain range trailed off to the north from Pikes Peak, concluding with Longs Peak, which was very high, and Mount Elbert, which was highest of all.

The lure of these mountains was irresistible. My brother Frank and I would join up with the Squires young men and drive a team and spring wagon with our tent and supplies and, perhaps, we would take along a pack horse or two just to be on the pioneer side. We would make the 30 mile trip to the beginnings of the mountains, and then we would go up into those beautiful pine-covered Rocky Mountains to find a clear, sparkling-clean stream and a grassy place to pitch our tent, feed our horses, build a fire, cook our dinner, and sleep for the night. There was always an uneasy feeling that our horses might stray away and that, maybe, a meandering bear would come our way. No such incident occurred, however. Other than some other minor incidents, we got along fine.

In later years we drove our cars into the mountains. We camped along the Platte River and along the various creeks that came down the frontal range. It was great fun, and we never tired of it. We were always glad, however, to get back to our ranch homes and join with our ranch families in the life we had known since childhood.

We often played baseball, and we dearly loved our Elbert team that competed with other teams from other towns. We had a great pitcher named Harvey Gatewood. He threw a very fast ball. One day, he accidentally hit a player in the head, and the player did not recover. Our great pitcher did not pitch another game. We had a remarkable second baseman named Everett Dittemore. He could leap into the air and catch a line drive with one hand. He was fast on double plays. We always cheered him.

One Sunday afternoon, a violent rainstorm came up and a team that had come from Denver to play against Elbert was stranded in the mud. We put them up at our house and let them sleep in the clean hay of our barn loft. My mother, bless her, fed the whole lot.

These were the lives of young ranchers in the early 20th century.

CHAPTER 14

Farming

After the range was enclosed, only those who had thousands of acres could continue with pasturing cattle and nothing else. The quest for income required ranchers to become farmers. They were already well on the way in this direction, since they were growing feedstuff, such as hay, oats and some corn.

They soon diversified into cash crops. Potatoes were very important in our part of Elbert County. They grew well, produced generously and brought quick money.

There were insects to plague the potato vines, and soon the particular nutrients which stimulated potato growth were depleated. But when I was a small child, I heard my father say that a person could buy a section of land and pay for it in three or four years by growing potatoes. They were of extremely high quality and readily marketable. In addition, they were very good in stimulating the soil for such crops as wheat and corn, which came on rapidly.

I grew up picking potatoes, and later I began cultivating corn and shocking wheat. The binder that cut the wheat and tied it into bundles was already popular by the time I could help around the place. Shocking wheat to avoid damage from rain and hail was a very difficult task. My oldest brother, Harvey, was very good at it. He handled two bundles at a time and made elegant shocks. Now and again we would see a field mouse scamper as we shocked the grain, but we saw them more often as we were pitching the bundles onto a hayrack to feed them into a thresher. Combines were unknown at that time.

My nephew, Bryce Gresham, tells me that wheat has come to be the major cash crop with the arrival of combines and highly mechanized preparation for marketing. One of the great joys of early ranch life was lost when we lost the old steam threshing machine. The thresher would pull his equipment from ranch to ranch and the wives would compete as to how well they could feed the threshers. The neighbors pitched in at each place, knowing that they would get help in return. Companionship was most pleasant and dinners for the harvest hands were a study in pioneer feasting. Neighboring wives would come in to help the hostess where the threshing machine was located, and there would be the most amazing display of fried chicken, fresh meat, potatoes, gravy, beans, peas, squash, cabbage, lettuce, and whatever else grew well in those rural gardens.

When the threshing was over, the farmers would count up the days for which they had traded and the days for which they owed cash money. As a boy in my early teens, I was humiliated when my father, in settling up, counted me as one-half hand. This was particularly frustrating when I knew I had produced more and better than any of the men on the job. I was somewhat comforted when my father explained to me that the other neighbors would not understand that, and they naturally expected a boy to be only half as valuable as a man.

As I developed into a young man, the farming became as interesting as the cattle ranching. It lacked, however, the mystique and lure of the old west, which made every Ranchland boy thrill when he started working with cattle.

CHAPTER 15

Religion

In the horse and buggy days the ranchers tended to have Sunday school and church services in clustered neighborhoods. There were even some churches in the wildwood, such as the Stone Church near where the Litherlands and the Phillipses lived. There was a time when services were held at the James School near the Cantrells. We attended a service of sorts at our own Lincoln School by our house. I could hardly wait for Sunday because the children played croquet on the school ground.

Many of us drove into Elbert for worship at the Presbyterian Church perched on the face of the hill. My father was an elder, and much respected by the members. He stumbled into trouble with some of the fierce predestinarians when he made a contribution toward the new Catholic Church that was under construction. Another elder mentioned in the session meeting that it was not proper for one of the elders to be supporting the Catholics. I was proud of my father, who said, "I may not spend my money as well as you would, but I spend it to suit myself. I believe in all of the churches." He was criticized no more. Both of my parents were members of that Presbyterian Church for the rolling years. Their funeral services were in that same building; my father died at 87 and my mother lived to be 93.

When I was about 11 or 12 years old, there came to town a Christian Church evangelist named C. M. Root. I heard his sermons with my brothers. There were many young people joining the Christian (Disciples of Christ) Church. I was deeply moved by the message, and went forward with some of my friends.

My brother Frank and I rode in to that Christian Church each Sunday on our saddle ponies. Our parents continued their active membership in the Presbyterian Church. These were the only two churches in town. Now I am old and have traveled the world and attended worship at St. Peter's in Rome and Westminster Abbey in London, but I have always been a member of some Christian Church. I found my religion in the Ranchland.

I shall never forget the day when I was baptized by immersion in Kiowa Creek. Jack Baldwin, a famous raconteur of the region, told me about the preacher who baptized in winter by cutting a hole in the icy stream. One candidate slipped from his hands and was carried away downstream. Unperturbed, the pioneer preacher said, "The Lord giveth and the Lord taketh away; bring on another brother." Nobody, including me, believed him.

After church services, families would go to visit neighbors for Sunday dinner. Fried chicken and homemade ice cream were very important in my young life. We children often waited until the adults had consumed a leisurely meal. The time dragged a bit for hungry children. One of the rituals of the Sunday dinner was the turning of the ice cream freezer. We had learned to save the ice by burying it in sawdust. I was proud when I could turn the handle. The dessert was homemade pie or cake with that wonderful ice cream. The country wives competed to see who could make the best. My mouth still moistens when I remember.

CHAPTER 16

The Automobile

The automobile brought change to the Ranchland. The small town merchants began to lose the most affluent trade to Denver and Colorado Springs. While these metropolitan centers were accessible by carriage, the time was long and the horses grew tired by the time they reached the destination. This meant a livery stable for the night and a hotel room for the travelers. All of this was expensive.

With the newfangled autos, the trip to and from in one day was very simple. Fords and Chevys were most popular, but some prosperous ranchers bought Pullmans, Studebakers, Buicks, Oldsmobiles, Dodges, Reos, Chandlers, Chalmers, Overlands, Maxwells, Essexes, Hudsons, Hupmobiles, Crow-Elkharts, and the very rich might even go for a Pierce Arrow. Everybody talked about cars and bragged about those that could reach the breakneck speed of 50 or 60 miles per hour. To climb the steep hill going west from Elbert in high gear was big stuff.

Rallies were planned from time to time as the cars became more numerous. Proud ranchers would gather to show off their cars. One of the most popular men in our area was an auctioneer who brought down the hammer at public auctions when a rancher decided to go somewhere else, or when the going got too rough and he ran for cover. Fred Albin appeared at one of these rallies with a Stutz Bearcat. This was the talk of the area. When I was old enough, I rebuilt a 1911 Ford into a speedster. It was great fun, but it looked homemade, which it was.

The sociology of the region in those early decades of the Twentieth Century shows the decline of the villages and the reduction of local social life. Instead of planning parties at various homes and exchanging visits with neighbors, the folk tended to drive into the city to shop and see a movie. The local stores, banks and service centers all felt the loss of patronage. Even the railroads began to close down. Shipping and passenger service had gone to the car and the truck.

There were no driver's licenses required. I owned my own car by age 12. Working with ranch machinery, I was a qualified driver. Building my own car made me into a fairly good mechanic. Cars were simple then, and common sense served well for repairing and maintaining our vehicles.

By the time I was 16, I had graduated to a red Buick roadster. It was a most satisfactory car, and I drove it until I left the ranch to go to Denver for schooling. I missed my saddle horse and my riding gear much more than I missed that red ragtop.

CHAPTER 17

Hunting

The Ranchland young people grew into the lore of the West as naturally as children who live by an ocean feel the lure and magic of the sea. Hunting, for us, was a lingering quest for food to put on the table. When I was old enough to have a .22, I began to shoot cottontails. My mother required that I dress them and prepare them for cooking. When I was old enough to handle a shotgun, I brought down many ducks. Once again, I was required to prepare them for cooking. I had trouble with the plucking, for some of the downy feathers were almost invisible, as well as difficult to remove. Mother solved my problem by teaching me to skin the ducks; she said the skin was not good for us. How she knew about cholesterol is still a mystery to me.

I was proud of my guns; first a Winchester single-shot .22 and, much later, a 30-caliber trombone-action Remington. My shotgun was a prize Ithaca double-barrel with a beaded rib for sighting. When canvas-backs, pin-tails and mallards gathered around what we called "buffalo wallows," I bagged my share of waterfowl. None was wasted; if I had too many for our family, I shared the game with neighbors. Neighbors in the Ranchland, though located miles apart, were very good about sharing. I remember when a child from a nearby ranch (a mile away was nearby) brought some food and said to my mother, "We just couldn't eat this!" Mother was amused, for she knew what the child meant.

Deer were scarce then in our section of the country. I went up into the mountains in search of venison, but with meager success. When it came to coyotes, I did much better. We regarded them as enemies of our young animals.

I loved turkey shoots and won a few prizes. I had a saddle scabbard for my deer rifle, and carried it as I rode. I always kept a .22 in my car.

Prairie chickens were around, but not numerous. The early settlers had about wiped them out as did the English with the now extinct bustards of East Anglia. I bagged a few with pride, rather than with the more appropriate sense of shame; I had no idea that they were an endangered species. My grandnephews tell me that prairie chickens are now very rare in the entire region.

My closest encounter with a large cat came on a very snowy day when, through the ice crystals, we spotted what we thought to be a lynx. The ears were much like the pictures in the outdoor magazines. He lifted one foot as he surveyed the threat, concluded we were enemies, and retreated into the snowstorm. My dreams of a lynx coat for my mother faded.

CHAPTER 18

Electricity, Mail and Telephones

In my boyhood, we had no electricity and, at first, we did what everybody did — lived with oil lamps and an occasional carbide lamp when we needed unusual light. We also had a gasoline lamp which we had to pump up so that the gas was diffused through a little gauze mantle of carbide. This gave a brilliant light. Lights of this variety are still used in camping.

I was still a small boy, however, when my father bought a Delco system. The gasoline engine turned the generator which charged the batteries and provided the supplemental electricity for the lights, which my father had arranged for both the house and the barn. That was a great day and made life easier for everybody, especially my mother.

I had left the ranch before the REA came in to supply electricity to everybody — everybody, that is, except our wonderful neighbor, Jim Dittemore. He refused the electric lights because they were "newfangled, dangerous and unnecessary."

Electricity for the Ranchland was an enormous benefit. It made life much easier, but it also hastened the drift toward the cities, for people read more and grew less content with their homemade fun, homemade amusements and homemade most everything. Today, the custom-made is premium. That day, the "store-bought" was choice and the custom-made disparaged.

When I was a boy, we had to ride a horse or drive a team four miles to Elbert to get the mail from our mailbox in the post office. RFD came to the Ranchland at about the same time as I departed, for I clearly remember having a mail box with a flag on it and going out to get the mail. Today, mail service is a family matter, since my nephew, Warren Gresham, is now the postmaster in Elbert.

Telephone was new in my days at the ranch. The neighbors all pitched in to provide the lines that would carry the telephone calls. For some difficult areas we managed to use the barbed wire of the fence, but mostly we put up two-by-fours and attached plain wire using insulators to avoid grounding. The telephone in our house was fastened to the wall and had to be cranked to call out. Each subscriber had a particular ring, such as a long, two shorts and a long, for we had party lines. It was generally accepted that almost everybody "listened in." Our telephone operator was Tiny Griffin. She could be very sharp as she handled the old plug-in switchboard, and if a person didn't talk to suit her, she disconnected.

These communication arrangements sound primitive today, but they were new and wonderful then. They brought much happiness to some wonderful people who made that pioneer west into a primitive paradise for children like me and the other members of my family.

CHAPTER 19

Parties

Our social life was largely homegrown, the same as our vegetables and our other provisions such as poultry, beef, pork and lamb. One rancher would give a party, and we would all gather 'round to play such party games as "Post Office," "Scissors" and "Beast, Bird Or Fish."

More often, we danced "The Virginia Reel," "Skip To My Lou," and "Through The Window." We did some square dancing and had some expert callers.

From time to time, we would meet at our Lincoln School for a dance. It was there I first learned to waltz, not very gracefully, but at least with a clear conception of the 3/4 time. We used Victrola music mostly, but occasionally we had our own volunteer band made up of Clyde Deremo, the Squires boys, my brother Frank and one or two others.

Now and again we would have a box social.

The belles of the region would prepare lovely decorated feasting goodies, such as cakes and pies, and often a complete gourmet dinner. A good auctioneer would pick up those lovely decorated offerings and call for bids. The person who bid the most would get to eat with the young lady who had prepared the food.

Don't tell me the Ranchland life was without its fun and games!

CHAPTER 20

Dropping Out of School

One of the big events in my life came when I first started high school. The nearest high school was in Elbert, four miles away, and I had to either walk or ride my saddle pony. I usually rode my pony. It worked out very well in the autumn, until the weather turned cold and bad, as it does in that high country; then I began to worry about my saddle pony. I had provided oats for his lunch in a nosebag, but I could not provide shelter. One day, when the northwest wind howled over the hills and canyons, I decided to give up high school and take my pony home where he could be warm and comfortable.

I can never forget the sadness in the face of the principal, Mr. Morrison, when I gave him my decision. He said, "Perry, you are one of the best students I have. We'll miss you." Well, I missed him and the classes. I loved Latin and algebra, English, geography and history; but, a decision was a decision, and my pony meant more to me. At home I borrowed a team and wagon from my father and found work hauling sand for the county dirt roads. It was very hard work, but I made good money. With about $18 a day for team, wagon and equipment, I soon became what I then considered to be rich. I lived at home, with no expense, and saved every penny of it.

I was also successful in developing a small herd of cattle. My father gave me a heifer when I was very small, and I soon bred, from her and her offspring, a fine little herd, even though I sold off some of the cattle for a nice profit. I soon had enough money to buy a handsome second-hand red Buick convertible. They were not called "rag-tops" then; they were called "roadsters."

That was my car in which I did my first courting and in which I eventually drove to Denver to school. Therein hangs another tale.

CHAPTER 21

Discourse of the Early Ranchland

The Ranchland of my youth had some colorful expressions which I have heard but seldom, if at all, since those days. "Howdy, pardner!" or "Howdy, stranger!" were common greetings. Today the likely greeting is "How ya doin'?". The usual mode of expressing gratitude then was "'preciate it" or "much obliged." Here are a few cliches of my youth which I hear no more:

- Strong as a young bull;
- Flighty as a stud horse;
- Squealed like a stuck pig;
- Jumped around like a chicken with its head cut off;
- Weak as a cat;
- Sly as a coyote;
- Noisy as a bunch of magpies;
- Ran like a scairt rabbit;
- Nervous as a wolf bitch in heat;

- Mad as a wet hen;
- Happy as a meadowlark;
- The very audacity. (I have no foggy notion of the origin. It was an exclamation expressing astonishment and disapproval.)
- High muckety mucks. (Highly placed persons; if they were pretentious, they were called "high falutin'!")

A person who acted in a stupid fashion might be called a "sap" or a "saphead." He might also be called "looney" or "batty." The old rancher would call him "locoed." (Loco is a Ranchland plant which was believed to, when eaten, cause the livestock to go wild.)

A former acquaintance who was not recognized might be addressed, "I didn't know you from Adam's off ox."

A person might be regarded as "poor as Job's turkey."

A horse of low quality might be called "crow bait" or "bag of bones."

Instead of teasing someone, we "guyed" him. Early ranchers might say we "rawhided" him, or on occasion, we "hoo-rahed" him.

"She came at me just a faunchin" meant to show agitation and anger. Instead of fussing at each other we "jawed" one another.

"Don't holler till you're hurt" was a bit of wisdom for one who borrowed trouble.

"Nix on the chin goods" was a pleasant way to say "shut up."

"Independent as a hog on ice" was a way to describe a person who was in a predicament but still would have his own way.

"His car came sleddin' down the hill" was used to say his brakes locked.

"Don't go rammin' in!" was advice to one who would take precipitous action.

Anything worthless was "not worth a hill of beans."

CHAPTER 22

Twilight Memories

Sixty-five years have rolled by since I packed my clothes into the trunk of my Buick roadster and headed down the dirt road toward Denver. I have returned on several occasions, but only to visit. My Ranchland boyhood seems far away and long ago. My memories, however, are vivid and lasting.

Most of all, I remember my family with whom the atmosphere was warm and cheerful. My father was widely respected in the region, and my mother was the essence of intelligent love. How she ever managed to accomplish all of the things she did to rear four children and tend the chores, at the same time able to take her place in the social structure of the community, is more than I can comprehend. She must have been a genius. My siblings were wonderfully caring and helpful to their little brother.

Next, I remember Pikes Peak which loomed

as a giant wedgewood monument to the land and its people. The peak was white in winter and purple in summer, but blue and white in between. It is the salient landmark of the entire region, forever beckoning and always challenging. From its summit came the notable song, "America The Beautiful," from the pen of Katherine Lee Bates.

The flowers and trees with the animals and the birds still come before my eyes. The quaking aspen grove on the Epler ranch, owned by my grandmother, is especially sacred in my memory. There we gathered for picnics; there my name was inscribed in the bark of one of the trees. The columbines appeared in that grove when gentle summer came to the Ranchland.

I loved the flags in the lowlands and the Indian paint brush on the hills. The bluebells, the larkspur, the daisies and the wild peas are deep in my recollection.

The hawks, magpies, skunks and weasels were our enemies because they threatened our fowl and our infant pets. But they were so beautiful that I loved them anyway. The coyote, in like fashion, was our enemy; but I remember him as a wily creature that commanded my respect. The bluebirds of my childhood were a study in grace, beauty and color. The peewee was a cheerful harbinger of springtime. The snowbird was a perpetual delight, and I was filled with wonder as the echelons of geese flew noisily by. I remember a cloud of bobolinks rising from the millet patch and a meadowlark on a fence post sounding his stentorian call across the fields of undulating wheat.

I remember the grama grass waving in the prairie breeze. The vast fields of wheat ready for harvest and the field of corn for ensilage or ripening are among the things I have loved. Great loads of hay to be lifted into the big red barns, and the fields of oats and alfalfa to feed the livestock in the long winter; these are lingering memories.

When I close my eyes I can see again the little green schoolhouse where I began my academic pilgrimage. It still stands, and I love it!

Growing up in the Ranchland was a great privilege, and I would not trade that beginning for marble halls and storied palaces!

CHAPTER 23

Pranksters

Halloween was a big evening for the Ranchland youth. Parents might take the smaller children to the closer ranch houses or to some school or church occasion where they could show off their masks and receive apples or homemade candy. Sometimes they would really bob for apples in a large tub of water and some talented adult would tell scary ghost stories.

The teen-age boys, however, were out for pranks. They would play visiting goblins to the entire neighborhood. Standard pranks consisted of upsetting the outhouses. When I was older and in college it was said in fun that one of our football players had B.O. so bad that every Halloween the other players would tip him over!

Boys from our neighborhood were creative. At one home they took a buggy apart and reassembled it on top of the barn! Sometimes the marauders would concoct stink bombs to annoy the neighbors. At one ranch they took the harness off the hooks and piled it at another place in the barn. Occasionally they would not be content with tipping over the privy; they would carry it away to some inconvenient distance. Other times they would be content to make weird and ghostly noises to awaken the neighbors.

Writing derogatory words on the schoolhouse windows about the teacher was not uncommon. Mostly they wrote with soap, but bad boys used candles. When the automobile came to the area, the windows were in for some Halloween scribbling.

There was very little trick-or-treat exchange. Now and then a family would be waiting for the tricksters and invite them in for cider or coffee. The homemade cinnamon rolls made all the trouble worthwhile and spared the trickery.

For the most part, the young were not vandals. I knew of one case in which they disconnected the main wire to the distributor on a man's new Ford car. As soon as he opened the hood he could spot the reason his car would not start. I knew of nobody sprinkling tacks, but I did know of a case in which some roughies let the air out of a tire.

Sometimes a family would plan a Halloween party which would provide a happy alternative to trickery. I remember a few such parties that were great fun for everybody.

CHAPTER 24

Winter

When the northwest wind began to sweep down from the Rocky Mountains, I found rare happiness in the anticipation of winter. I loved the snow, and though I feared the blizzards, I welcomed the onset of winter. I greatly enjoyed all the preparations which ranch life required.

When I was small I worked with my mother to bring in the vegetables from the garden. We packed carrots, onions, beets and parsnips in sand or in sawdust in the cellar of our house. Mother canned the tomatoes, beans, peas and the fruit which my father brought home from Denver or Colorado Springs. I helped to peel peaches; especially when she placed them in hot water so the skin would slip away from the fruit.

As I grew older I helped to prepare wood for the stove using saw and axe as needed. I even helped my father butcher the animals for pork, beef and lamb. Scraping a hog was a particularly difficult operation. I created much amusement in my family when I thought that pork chops came from the jowls. Skinning a beef was dangerous business, and I was permitted no part in it until I was a sizable youth.

Most of our winter wardrobe came from two sources: Sears & Roebuck and Montgomery Ward. I selected sheep-wool-lined boots and tall four-buckle overshoes. I had a sheepskin coat that lasted for many seasons. It was too big for me at first, but in a couple of years I grew into it. I luxuriated in the blanket sheets for my bed.

Ranchland men wore blue denim overalls with a bib and straps. Each one had a Sunday suit; usually of blue serge which wore like iron and shined with age. When a tear occurred, my mother used mending tape to patch the place. She always darned our socks, and used a plain old washboard to keep her brood clean and tidy. She always ironed our shirts, heating the iron on the kitchen range. How she managed all of these things is now a mystery.

The livestock became more animated with cold weather. Their fur grew thick and they looked more contoured. My saddle horse seemed to love the cold weather as much as I did. I carried a pocket full of oats to reward him when he came at my call.

I helped to bring corn and hay into the barn. This would see the livestock through the winter cold and snow.

CHAPTER 25

Community

Ranchland people really care about one another; at least they did when I was a growing lad. Our homes were far apart, but our hearts were together.

Roy Squires lost an arm in an agricultural accident. Only the help of caring neighbors and an alert and devoted family saved his life. He was in the hospital for a long time. The spring planting was neglected.

On the appointed day a miracle occurred. Just as the rose glow of dawn touched the Pikes Peak, there was a team and implement or a tractor and implement on every hilltop even though the neighbors came from far away. With the skill and experience of men who knew what they were doing, the fields of Roy Squires were ploughed, harrowed and sown — all in one day! Even when well and in possession of both arms, it would have required that Roy spend several weeks at the operation. Those strong men cared about one another and were willing to lend a hand, no matter how busy.

Ed Clarke, our closest neighbor, lost his comfortable ranch house in a fire. We came from all directions to help. It was too late to extinguish or even control the blaze. We all tried to save as many things as we could without immolating ourselves. I was but a brash boy, but I rushed in to grab a few things such as a sewing basket and a gasoline lamp. My hands were scorched and I smelled like a singed fowl, but I felt very proud. Food, lodging and clothing were supplied by the neighbors until arrangements were made and the building replaced.

At haying time and threshing we helped one another. There were no combines then. A steam-powered threshing machine moved from place to place as needed. We converged on the location so that the owner could keep the hungry machine busy. Each neighbor brought his own team and hayrack. The wheat, oats or barley had been cut with a binder and placed in shocks with the grain heads up so the shock could be capped with one or two bundles. This kept the rain from doing too much damage, but it was best to get the thresher there before rains came.

All of us would fan out into the field and load our wagons so that we could keep a steady line pulling up to the feeder of the thresher. It was hard and demanding work, but I loved it. I was very young, but I carried my full load. My wagon was full and in line when my turn came. The women came to prepare the dinner (always at noontime). Those were feasts to remember!

CHAPTER 26

The Charivari

We spelled the name of the mock concert for a newly married couple "chivaree". That was our pronunciation as well. It was a curious and widely-practiced custom brought over from the Continent. I have not heard the name or known of the practice in years. The event varied with the imagination and inventiveness of the friends.

After the wedding, which was held either in the home of the bride or at a church, the young friends would prepare some outlandish sounds to annoy the young couple on their wedding night. We worked at the business of creating strange and frightening sounds. We made a unique noisemaker by whittling saw-tooth notches on the collars of a spool. We would wind twine around the area once filled with thread and insert a pencil through the cylinder. By holding the pencil parallel with a window and pulling on the twine we created a rattling roar to disturb the bride and groom. Other disturbers brought old tin pans to beat on. These sounds, enhanced by discordant whoops, ringing cow bells and shouting, would wake the dead.

The victims of the prank were savvy. They were expecting us. They appeared fully clothed and invited us in for coffee and cinnamon rolls as well as popcorn. We soon departed, since ranch people tended to be in the fields or in the saddle at daybreak.

Weddings today are shockingly expensive, costing the bride's family thousands of dollars. Ranchland weddings were simple and very attractive. There were no black ties nor expensive gowns for the bride's attendants. The bride herself, with the help of her mother, provided the beautiful gowns, some of them relics from parents and grandparents. The men wore "Sunday go-to-meetin'" suits with white shirts and exuberant ties. A stick-pin and a flower were in order. The place was decorated with flowers from local gardens. It was very striking — enough so to strike envy to a florist.

The wedding reception was usually at the family home of the bride or at the church social rooms. Bouquets were thrown, the cake was ceremoniously cut, and toasts were given. Some customs never change.

Opulent grooms gave six dollars to the preacher.

CHAPTER 27

Throwaways

"The Gambler" was one of the most popular songs of Kenny Rogers. One telling line in the lyric is, "Every gambler knows the secret of survival is knowing what to throw away and knowing what to keep." My life would have been richer and better if I could have known and practiced that wise maxim.

Treasures of those pioneer days are gone forever. Where now is my stock saddle? My russet leather bridle with silver rosettes is long forgotten. These little baubles mean little, although I do wish I had saved that Navajo saddle blanket. Saved items that would mean something today include our 1918 Maxwell and that luxurious phaeton coach. Where Dad acquired that handsome rig I do not know. I only know that it was the marvel of the neighborhood; so much so that our modest family felt out of place riding in it. Besides, we had no liveried driver to sit in the high seat while the aristocrats were in robes and cushions in the main compartment.

This expensive conveyance sat idly in back of the granary. We had the idea of cutting the body and making it into a sled. We improvised wooden runners with strap metal tires for sliding. The result was an attractive, unique and very heavy sled. It required a powerful team of horses to pull it, and it was extremely difficult when we came upon a patch of road where the snow had exposed the muddy ground. I drove it a few times, but it was not one of my better ideas. Oh, if I had had sense enough to put it under cover and save it for a museum piece!

We traded in our old Maxwell for a pittance; now it would be a classic worth thousands of dollars. The fine old wagons weathered away in the scrap pile until my parents were gone and the house was vacant. Collectors stole the wheels of all of our implements and conveyances to use them for Western gates and fences in their citified homes. Perhaps they did not think of it as stealing, but rather as collecting. They collected everything inside and outside the buildings, except the kitchen sink. It was not much good and all used up!

I saved a few things, such as pride and pleasure in the land of my boyhood. I still remember the aroma of the livestock, the leather of my saddle, the thrill of my running quarter horse, the pleasure of driving four horses tandem, my first car, and the everlasting love and friendship of my family and friends.

CHAPTER 28

Television Comes
To The Ranchland

I was long gone from the Ranchland when
television came. I saw my first television in
London shortly after the war. I was living at the
Authors Club that summer, and I found the
lounge. It was always silent and almost empty,
filled with members who were quite awed with the
images of the Changing of the Guard as they
appeared on the screen of the new contraption.

When I returned to Detroit, television was
already there. We purchased a new set, which
was then quite expensive, and told our Colorado
family about the new marvel. They were already
getting the broadcasts from the top of Cheyenne
Mountain near Colorado Springs. A man named
Jim Russell came on each day to explain the
marvels and mysteries of television. He and his
wife, Betty, had purchased KVOR, The Voice of the
Rockies, which was a somewhat neglected radio

station. They had rehabilitated it, and when opportunity came, they applied for the first television channel in Colorado. Denver objected, but the Russells, with the spirit of Old Kentucky, prevailed. They came on the air as KKTV, a CBS station. My family loved it and always tuned in.

Imagine my delight and surprise when Jim and Betty became my new neighbors at Bermuda Village, where we live part time on account of my health. Jim has emphysema and I have cancer and heart difficulties, but we are of the same pioneer stock and we keep on going. We are both fortunate to have such resilient wives. Betty takes care of Jim and Aleece takes care of me. We have a great time talking about our Colorado days and sharing the *Ranchland News.*

Television has come a long way since those early days. Jim and Betty sold the station and moved to the land of lotus eaters. The station has changed owners several times since then, but my family still watches the station and remembers Jim.

When I visit my families who live around Elbert, I am impressed with the fact that their reception is even better than we have at Bethany. The vast plains carry the image much better than our mountains. Cable has made good images even better. I frequently enjoy the comfort of home while viewing the world news and the most exciting sporting events.

Our friendship with the Russells enables me to understand, somewhat, the trials and tribulations involved in opening and operating a new station. Some of my friends are always knocking the tube. It is a great source of help and enjoyment for me, and it keeps me informed about the exciting world in which we live.

Faith Daniels does the news on NBC, and we seldom miss her report. She is a graduate of Bethany College, and all Bethanians and many Mountaineers walk in proud shoes because of her fame and ability. She returns often to Bethany and is as proud of us, as we are of her!

CHAPTER 29

Travel

On recent visits to the Ranchland, I remembered the dirt roads of my boyhood as I drove on paved roads to Simla, Calhan, Elizabeth and Elbert in a powerful modern car. I parked at church and noticed the Cadillacs, Buicks, Toyotas, Volvos, Fords and Chevrolets; I remembered when the parking lot was mostly hitching posts and the person who drove in with a newfangled car had to be careful not to scare the horses.

Those dirt roads were a problem. In wet weather they developed deep ruts. By the time I was a teenager we had graveled the most traveled highways and many of the county roads. Dust was everywhere, but we were not alarmed. We thought good clean dust was good for us. It must have been; many of us have lived well beyond the fourscore years allotted by the Psalm.

Through the haze of memory, I am astonished at the courage of my parents, who threw a water bag over the radiator spout, packed a supply of food and drink, tied a tent on the spare tire and set out for California. Paved roads were rare. When we finally came to the desert area, my father let some of the air out of the tires so we would not mire down in the sand, and we traveled cross-country with only a map and an occasional landmark to guide us. We arrived, but not even on a Far Out expedition would I undertake it today.

How fondly I remember setting up the tent and making the campfire. We were unafraid of molesters; everyone minded his own business. There were but few people on the road. Frequently we found lodging and food in a small town along the way. Flat tires were not uncommon. We jacked up the wheel, removed the tire from the rim with a tire iron, and patched the inner tube with some prepared material which vulcanized the area of the leak. I was the smallest member of the family and was spared much of the hardship.

When we reached California we were with family. I loved the pepper trees and the orange groves. The eucalyptus was fascinating and I saved the nuts for decorations. My mother made a portiere of them by putting them on strings and hanging them in rows to fill the doorway.

Coming home to Colorado was the best. I had missed my pony and the pets. Never was there a sweeter redolence than my mother preparing supper on our own kitchen stove. Soup ladled from a large central bowl was life at its best!

CHAPTER 30

Barbecues

Among the happy memories of my boyhood are the big barbecues provided by some well-to-do ranchers or by some political campaign; occasionally by some company or organization. As I remember, it was like this:

The host would dig a pit several feet deep and rectangular in shape. The sides would be lined with sheet metal to reflect the heat inward. A grate would be prepared to protect the meat from burning. The pit would be large enough to accommodate a whole pig or sheep, but a side of beef would be cut into two or three parts. County Sheriff Roy Brown was usually among the experienced hands who would tend the cooking contents, using a pitch fork. When the meat was well cooked it would be lifted with appropriate tongs and covered with barbecue sauce. When sliced and placed on a round bun it was yummy!

People came from miles around. Each

family would bring its own basket of potato salad, pickled beets and peaches, wilted lettuce, pork and beans (Van Camps), potatoes and ears of corn. On some occasions the corn and beans were part of the gift to the public. The variety of pies and cakes would tempt the Olympian gods!

This Ranchland feast was always at noon (what we called dinner). The young, including me, would be entertained by a well-planned field day. How well I remember the three-legged race. Two boys, standing side-by-side, would put one leg into a sack so that each would have a free leg, but the other two would be tied together so that in the race there were but three legs. Running in that condition required much coordination and not a few spills.

Horseshoe pitching was the sport of the older men, while the young ones played softball or competed in the races, wrestling or eating contests. The eating contests were usually planned for watermelon, which could then be bought for a quarter or less.

A political address or some singing was not unusual. In case the sponsor was a church there would be a sermon. Sometimes the church leaders were practical enough to take up a collection!

The site was usually a wooded area where there was plenty of shade where the women could gossip or discuss the problems of gardening or canning. This was a real old-time chuck wagon feast, and boy, was it fun! I can still taste the barbecue and the ubiquitous lemonade!

CHAPTER 31

Work

In my boyhood the word "industry" meant habitual hard work. I was industrious when I carried my part of the chores and the daily work on the ranch. Today the word industry connotes manufacturing. An industrialist is a person highly-placed in manufacturing.

When the founding fathers of our nation lived by the puritan virtues of honesty, frugality and industry they had reference to hard and habitual work. They spoke of a young man as "industrious" if he performed his various tasks with attention and sufficient effort to get things done. He was the opposite of lazy.

We have now a generation in which work is often considered to be a curse we must endure to live. The joy and satisfaction of hard work is almost a casualty of our mechanized age. My academic colleagues talk about workaholics, as if a person who works hard and keeps at it has some kind of a bad habit like drinking or smoking. The job of working and doing a good job seems to be lost.

The best people I have known and with whom I have been associated have been hard workers. They had enough sense and perspective to avoid missing the attention, thought and creativity that goes into any important task. They had something of the quality of Sir Isaac Newton who, when asked how he arrived at his theory of gravity, answered, "By always attending to it." That strong Latin verb "teneo" implies stretching. He said in effect that he succeeded because he was forever stretching his mind toward it.

I have had many students who failed and who ruined their health by worry, or by some bad habit such as drinking or carousing, but I know of nobody who died of work. I do not intend to imply that a person should be a drudge. Everybody must find the rhythm of life which alternates work with rest and new perspectives. The archer hits the target, partly by pulling the bow string and partly by letting go. The successful mountain climber takes time out when he can to catch his breath and look around. But nobody hits the target or climbs the mountain by avoiding work.

Perhaps some people would call me a workaholic. I prefer to be called a hard worker. I agree with Carlyle when he said, "A man's work is his life preserver."

When someone says dourly, "I have to work today," I always say, "You are fortunate; keep at it!"

CHAPTER 32

Neckties

My mother always added a necktie when she dressed me in knickers and white shirt. When I was a bit older, she let me select my own necktie. Dad took me to Robbins On The Corner in Colorado Springs, where I selected a beauty. Harvey, my older brother, was along, and chose a more expensive tie for himself. I was very proud.

About a week later, when we were getting ready to go to some Ranchland function which involved my being "dressed up," I went for my new tie. When I put it on, Harvey insisted that it was his tie. I made a fuss and won permission. As would happen, I spilled some gravy on it. I felt bad about it, but when I returned home I found my new necktie in place. It was Harvey's new tie I had soiled! He was generous and forgiving, but I felt like a stupid little ass.

Neckties are a curious development of human decoration. My learned friends in anthropology tell me that homo sapiens began wearing clothes for decoration. The factor of warmth was a secondary consideration. The necktie is a late development which serves no useful function. Yet, ties are a social requirement in many, if not most, cultures. From boyhood on I always wore a tie with pride, but from time to time, they get spots of misdirected food. My neighbor, Ambrose Cram, says he spilled so many things on one necktie that he had to keep it in the refrigerator!

Neckties are out of fashion more often than other clothing. I have saved neckties from long ago, hoping that the cycle of style would bring them back; no such luck. Some are wide, some are narrow; some are long, others short; some are loud while others are subdued. In my boyhood, gentlemen always wore black ties at funerals. Even that expression of respect and mourning has long gone. If my mother were alive today, she would make a quilt of my collection.

I have bows and four-in-hand, subdued and exuberant, plain and fancy, but none coordinates with my new suit! Perhaps the dress codes of my boyhood should have given way to the informality of the later generations. Yet, I fondly remember when I could get rid of those pesky knickers, wear long pants and don a handsome necktie. At one time I wore a starched white shirt with detachable collar; some of my father's friends wore celluloid collars with pearl buttons! There was something noble about the strong rough men I knew as community leaders.

Life requires some ritual and dignity. I hope the necktie, or some equivalent, will prevail!

CHAPTER 33

Every Day on the Ranch

At school, at home, at church or at the store we gathered around the potbellied stove. There we removed our sheepskin coats, our caps with pull down tabs that protected our ears, our sheepskin gloves, and maybe our overshoes. On a cold winter day the temperature would go down below zero. When possible we had blankets for our horses.

Among objects long forgotten and seldom mentioned are oblong boilers for the Monday wash. Hand cranked wringers and corrugated washboards are seldom used since ranchers enjoy the latest equipment in electric washers and dryers. The old churn with a crock in which to operate a plunger is a casualty of modernity. Milk then was sold for the butter fat; cream rose to the top and often was churned into butter. Even the rolling pin is less ubiquitous today. Comics called them "husband trimmers;" that joke would fall flat with the modern generation. Rolling pins are rare.

Clothing has evolved. Ranchers in my day bought suits with two pair of pants; on very cold days they wore both of them! Every proper young lady had a fur muff. Each family enjoyed the comfort of a soapstone foot warmer which had a cover something like a tea cozy. We often wore leggings that laced around the calves of our legs to ward off the chill. Our overshoes were four-buckle or even six-buckle to protect as we walked in deep snow. A man's purse was usually a pouch with a draw string or a leather container with a metal device to keep it secure. Two or more compartments kept the bills separated from the change which was often silver dollars.

Everybody had a buggy whip. Some of them were highly decorated and made of covered rawhide. Each one had a colored tassel. I dearly loved to go to Denver with my father and visit the H. H. Heiser Harness and Saddlery Store on Larimer Street, where they were sold. As automobiles became more popular, one of the Heiser sons became a car dealer; the other son stayed on and sold to the rapidly diminishing market. Tractors replaced the Percheron, the Clydesdale and the Belgian. Draft horses and the cars reduced the market for buggy harness. Saddlery became a luxury for those who kept quarter horses or played cowboy for sport.

Those were the days!

CHAPTER 34

Patriotism

The Ranchland community was patriotic. I remember the young men marching and volunteering for the First World War. As a small boy I made a wooden gun with a hand saw and a piece of one-by-four board.

The presidential race was between Woodrow Wilson and Charles Evans Hughes. I remember the slogan of Wilson's campaign, "A vote for Wilson is a vote for peace." My father was unpersuaded and voted for Hughes, but Wilson won. The pacifism of the President did not keep us from going to war. The young men of the area enlisted. I marched with my wooden gun and wished I could be old enough to go to war.

Everybody believed in America. There was no flag burning and no downgrading of our Nation. The party out of the White House did not disparage our native land in order to mount a campaign for the next election. The wise ranchers

were working together for the good of the Nation.
The Denver Post and the *Rocky Mountain News*
were both backing the President who had, with
great reluctance, led us into an overseas war.

Now that I am old I see the naivete of the
widely quoted slogan, "A war to end all war." In
just over a score of years we were in another
World War which was more fierce and deadly. I
was much too young during the first world
encounter to realize that wars are in the nature of
humans. I was old enough to wonder why my
older friends had to die on the battlefields of
France. I sang the songs with gusto and belief,
but I have never ceased to wonder why we cannot
find some better way. Wilson's League of Nations
was a right idea, without adequate backing. Given
the nature of humanity, it may not be possible.

The proud individualism of Colorado
ranchers continues, but the Nation is torn with a
tendency toward excessive adversarial attitudes
and commitments. Government has multiplied
and taxes are burdensome. As Will Rogers said,
"Think of the cost of government today and it is
not one whit better than when we paid very little!"
He said, also, "Thank God we don't get all the
government we pay for!"

CHAPTER 35

The Stock Show

The Great Western Stock Show in Denver was a ranch boy's dream come true. My father was as keen on attending as I was. My sister and brothers were all about other things, but I had the privilege of going to Denver with my parents for the major event of the rancher's year.

We were to go by train. The C&S railway was still carrying passengers. We drove into Elbert and caught the train. The coach was almost empty. I found that I could reverse one seat back and form a compartment so that two seats faced each other. There we sat watching the pleasant countryside go by with its occasional ranch house, its cattle and horses, and its clusters of jack pine. When we came into the irrigated valley near Parker, I saw the fine big dairy barns and the prosperous-looking houses. At last the outskirts of Denver appeared.

We checked in at the Albany Hotel. Dad

knew most of the other guests, which lead me to believe this was the favorite spot for our neighbors. We were shown to our room, washed up a bit, and headed for the Stockyards.

I was fascinated by the beautiful cattle. Their horns and hooves were polished and their hair was neatly groomed. They were fat and contented with no foreknowledge of the fact that soon they might be beef. While Dad visited with his colleagues, I watched the judges at work as they made their decisions and passed out the ribbons.

For lunch I ate a hot dog and drank a creme soda pop. That fifteen cent repast tasted better to me than any of the thirty dollar snacks I, years later, enjoyed at the Waldorf Astoria. We visited the midway and headed for the hotel. We had tickets for a dinner theater where some fine singers presented a charming show — a sort of vaudeville production. The theme was Arabic and the song was "The Sheik." A beautiful lady sang "Hindustan." I was enthralled.

The next day brought the famous rodeo. The roping, bulldogging and the bronco busting were the best I had ever seen. I tried roping calves when I got home, but once I almost roped my own horse, the one on which I was riding!

Tired and still excited, on the next day we boarded the train for home. I had bought a new bridle with silver conchas. As we rode along I was munching on chocolate covered peanut clusters. Boy, were they good!

CHAPTER 36

Horses

A warm and friendly letter from Allen Peterson reminds me that horses are and have been the essence of the Ranchland. Allen should know. He has devoted his professional career to racehorse breeding. His famous "Little Beaver" won all of the prizes in the western states for his amazing speed. When "Little Beaver" was put down at last, Allen had a coat made of his hide.

When Allen dedicated his new horse barn he hosted a great barbecue and presided over a ceremony to remember. His horses, both quarter horses and thoroughbreds, are formidable in any racing event.

Automobiles, trucks, tractors and other powered machinery perform the transportation and do the work of farming and ranching, but the horse is by no means extinct. Perhaps there are more horses today than before the historic black Ford car made its successful debut. Every ranch and farm has a few horses for riding. They provide a most appropriate form of recreation and sport, as well as continue to serve the traditional function in driving, finding and attending the needs of livestock.

Allen tells a story of how my father asked his paternal grandfather if his fine stallion could breed one of the Gresham mares. Mr. Peterson agreed, and at the appointed time the animals were brought to Elbert. The eagerness of the stallion got out of hand and the event occurred right there in the center of town. Women hurried by, looking the other way.

Even ranch women were squeamish in those days. My grandmother would not even call the male bovine a "bull." She always euphemized the word to "gentleman cow!"

My favorite saddle horse was handicapped. He had a skeletal deformity which left one hip lower than the other. He made up in spirit what he lacked in natural conformation. He was the fastest horse in our neighborhood. Some horses, like people, seem to be born unlucky. This fine brave beast was, in his later years, victim of a careless neighbor who threw a rock at him and blinded one eye. With a twisted head and a hip knocked down he was still the best cow pony around! He taught me to care about the handicapped.

Our daughter and grandchildren are keen on horses. Our daughter, Nancy, especially, has won many blue ribbons and won many prizes in the hunt and in recreational riding. She always keeps a few fine saddle horses. I feel much at home around the creatures who gave adventure and happiness to my youth.

CHAPTER 37

Picnics

In the Ranchland, when the century was young, holidays meant picnics. We sometimes went to the aspen grove on Grandmother Epler's ranch or to Castlewood dam. There was a particular charm about Castlewood. We found water, which was in short supply on the sun-baked hills, we found trees which were shady and inviting, and we found picnic tables which spared us the problem of ants. There was a charm about the place which I remember with pleasant affection. We could improvise a softball field and there were iron stakes for horseshoes.

Our picnics were somewhat indigenous to the region. We almost always feasted on fried chicken, hard boiled eggs, Van Camp's pork and beans, homemade rolls and pickled beets. At times we had roasted ears of corn or roasted potatoes — all prepared on the spot with the campfire as the stove. Over cooked green beans with ham were common. I have not heard of pickalilly since those days. We often brought the ice cream freezer and the ice to wind up the meal with that delicious rich ice cream to which fresh fruit such as pineapple, peaches, cherries or strawberries had been added. Chocolate or coconut layer cake was usual; devil's food or angelfood were not uncommon. Everything was homemade.

Devil's Head was a bit farther away, but after we had better automobiles we often undertook the drive. That was about twenty or thirty miles away with a good stiff climb upon arrival. The view from the top made the trouble well worthwhile. Crowds were not a problem then. We were glad to see a few other people after our long days alone. That journey answered the call of the mountains and the challenge of a hill to climb. We were all young and strong with energy to spare.

One day at grandmother's grove I made a foolish mistake. I had brought my girlfriend from Denver to meet the family. I placed a can of beans in the campfire to get it warm before I opened it. The can exploded and spattered my lady friend with baked beans! I was both embarrassed and ridiculed.

Who said Ranchland life was no picnic?

CHAPTER 38

Watch Fobs and Stickpins

When the century was young, the watch fob and the stickpin were standard dress for the man of standing in the community. The watch fob made it easy for the rancher to withdraw his pocket watch. The fob was usually made of leather with some bit of ornamental metal at the end away from the watch. Some of them were fancied up with decorative jewels or ornaments. My brother, Harvey, said, "They made easy pickins for pick pockets". Railroad men were very proud of their open and shut pocket watches, and were proud of the watch fobs which withdrew the watch as they opened the face to reveal the exact time. This mattered much to railroaders.

Watch fobs and the much more valuable closed face watches are now among the most cherished of antiques. Some of them sell for thousands of dollars. Even some wrist watches which have largely displaced the old-time pocket watches are now valued in many thousands of dollars. The cheap watches of the old days were objects of ridicule, but antiquity has brought some astonishing value to them. Electric and self-wind watches of our time may be cheap, but just as accurate as were the expensive models of the days when the watch fob was still the style.

Before World War I, the well dressed man always wore a stickpin in his cravat (necktie). Some of them were quite valuable. They were set with precious stones, such as rubies and diamonds. More often they were tipped with gem stones, such as birthstones. Agates were very popular. I can tell you from personal experience that they were easy to lose. They gave, however, dash and character to the necktie of a rancher gentleman. I could hardly wait until I was old enough to wear one. I still have a small topaz which I saved from the days of my youth. When I dare to wear it, people think it must be my wife's scarf pin!

I can still see the distinguished men of the Ranchland with watch fobs and stickpins as they gathered to discuss the weather and new breeds of cattle. Change was always jingling in their pockets. Most of them smelled of cigars or pipes, but many "rolled their own." Chewing tobacco was very popular. I marvel that many men lived to ripe old age!

When my father went to the office of Governor Shoup on one occasion, he took me along. I still remember the size of the Colorado gold nugget which dangled from the Governor's watch chain. His stickpin was also a nugget. He was a portly man who preceded himself when he entered a room. Dad said he was a good governor. He looked almost like a god to a young lad from the country.

Who said men's styles never change?

CHAPTER 39

The Way We Were

Ranching and farming in those early days was much more rugged than it is today. The technological revolution has influenced the rural way of life. We did many things by hand that are mechanized today. Here are a few of the things I learned to do as a boy that are almost unheard of now.

We had mowing machines drawn by horses. The sickle needed sharpening from time to time, which was accomplished by a stone wheel or a hand tool. After the hay was cut, we allowed it to dry for a day or two before we moved in with a horse-drawn hay rake. When we worked frisky horses, these were dangerous occupations. I had a team run away when I was raking hay. The bumpy ride knocked me off the seat and down to where the tines were about to roll me over and over. I held on to the reins with the grit of a strong young country boy, and, by the grace of

God, the horses came to a standstill. I was fortunate enough to avoid an accident with the mower.

With the newly-mown hay in winrows, we would pile it in little stacks until it dried some more before we piled it on the hayrack. From there it went to the barn where it was lifted by a giant fork, or by a pre-placed sling, into the haymow. When there was no more room in the barn, we made haystacks that could withstand the wind, rain and snow. Sometimes we rented a hay baler which gathered up the winrows of hay and formed it into square bales tied with baling wire. The bales were heavy and hard to handle. The new round bales were then unknown.

I learned to repair harnesses. This included using a hand awl to punch the holes and some special strong thread that I waxed by hand. The wax was a ball sliced in half. I would carefully rub the string into the wax until it was completely covered and waterproof. Then I would thread it into some special needles, one at each end of a length of string, so that I could bring the two needles through the same hole in opposite direction. This, drawn tight, made a solid bind that would withstand the strain of a pulling horse. We would treat the harness in an appropriate oil to shed the water and keep the leather pliable.

Picking potatoes was one of my best achievements. At first we used a spading fork to lift the potatoes from the ground where they had grown. Then we would pick them up and put them in a sack prepared to hang from the shoulder. Later we had a potato digger, horse drawn, that would dig the spuds as it passed the row. Then I would come along with my potato sack and pick them up. I was good and fast. I learned to sort them for size as we went along.

These tasks are no more. You might call my youth wasted. I loved it!

CHAPTER 40

The Ways of the Wild

The ranch boy I once was comes often to my mind. I learned the ways of the wild.

It was a big revelation to me when I found out that the killdeer who seemed to be crippled and looked as if she had blood on her wing was actually putting on an act to lead me away from her nest. Later I tried to follow where she had been, to no avail. In all my childhood exploration I did not find the nest of a killdeer.

I did find the nest of a wild duck. She was a fairly tame wild duck who had learned to live around our pond. I thought she was a good friend. When her eggs were all in place, I thought it would be all right for me to lift her up the way I had lifted up a setting hen to peek at the eggs. The duck left the nest and did not return. That way I learned, sadly, the ways of the wild.

I once climbed a tall pine tree and found the egg of a hawk. Hawks were considered the enemies because they threatened our chickens. I very carefully put the egg in my pocket and climbed down the tree. The egg was beautiful. I put it in a little silver bowl in a nest of cotton. It was my proud decoration for the dining room until . . . one day it exploded while we were eating dinner! It was a foul stench. It interrupted the meal and caused me to hang my head in shame for several weeks until I could live down my gross error that not only deprived the hawk and deprived my family of their happy meal and the house of its pleasant aroma, but deprived me of my pride as a young naturalist.

I learned how cottontails hid in the rocks so that no one could see them. I found, to my horror, that some people took forked sticks and thrust them into the fur of the little rabbit to drag it out. We were, at that time, so near the pioneers that the rabbit was food for the table and fair game. It was my mother who taught me that animals have feeling, the same as I do.

I learned how the jackrabbit could hide himself in the snow so that nothing was visible except his eyes and his nostrils. It was a great camouflage, and it took sharp eyes to see him.

I learned, also, that the antelope had no ability to leap as did a deer. I noticed that the antelope always crawled under a fence instead of going over it. I found that they could go down flat like a limbo dancer.

Mule deer, now plentiful in the Ranchland, were scarce when I was a boy, but the one or two I saw on occasion enchanted me with the graceful leap that cleared the tall fence.

I learned the nature of the predators, such as the badger and the weasel. I learned how they prey upon other little animals. I saw a rabbit leaping in pain, but upon approaching, a weasel was holding onto his throat with a death grip and would not let go.

I heard the stories of how a porcupine could throw its quills. I have helped my dogs by pulling quills with a pair of pliers, but never did I suffer from a quill thrown at me by a porcupine.

When I grew a little older I asked my father how a porcupine could possibly make love.

He said, "Very carefully!"

CHAPTER 41

Mountains

When automobiles became popular, the Ranchland youth dearly loved to go to the mountains. Small wonder, because that mighty range looms blue in the sunlight, gray in the shadows and golden at sunrise. My brother Frank and I, along with Earl and Roy Squires, were often headed up into the mountains, usually over Ute Pass.

The Squires had a new Chevrolet. It had a cone clutch, which was very grabby. I was driving up a rather steep mountain. When I shifted down into low, I brought the gear into play too abruptly and it snapped the drive shaft. Not only was the power gone, but also the brakes!

The emergency brake was of little use. Here I was, going backward down a steep mountain. I saw an entering steep road on the right. The car was going too fast, but I made the turn backward up that other road until the car stopped and started frontward. I made the turn at the bottom and in two or three times rocked the car to a standstill. I felt relieved that I had saved four lives, but I felt terrible about the Squires' car.

Fortunately, the Squires' cousin, Barney, operated a very good garage in Eastonville. We had telephones then and were able to call him. He came up the mountain and towed the Squires' car back to his garage while we waited for him to get the needed parts and put it back together. I felt much relieved, but always guilty about damaging the Squires' car. I gladly offered to pay for the expense. They were unwilling to take it, but my father insisted and they reluctantly accepted.

We had other choice spots in the mountains. We loved South Park with its rolling acres of hay fields and its huge hay barns. We often drove along the Platte River and fished as best we could without much success. Trout were scarce in those days and there were no fisheries for stocking the streams.

We occasionally headed through Denver up Big Thompson Canyon to Estes Park. Especially in the spring or fall, we saw the herds of great elk that had come down from the mountains into the valley to feed. With field glasses we could see the mountain goats. The beautiful little lakes in Rocky Mountain National Park gave us enchantment.

One of our very favorite drives was to Mount Evans. The road was barely passable, but the view and the experience were worth all the trouble.

Frequently we took our own camping gear and simply put up a tent where we wanted to spend the night. We drank freely from the mountain springs with a belief that a few hundred yards over the stones would purify the water. None of us ever came down with any disease on account of it, but we know now our theory was not very scientific!

Each time I get out into the Ranchland now, I look at those mountains sweeping the skyline from Pikes Peak up to Longs Peak, and remember old times.

CHAPTER 42

Gardens

Among my most cherished boyhood memories are the flower gardens that gave fragrance and beauty to almost every ranch house and to the yards of those who lived in the Ranchland towns.

Among the flowers that were most prominent in our region were the morning glories on every fence. In back of them were the sweet peas, fragrant and colorful. At the appropriate season the gladioli came out. The iris grew wild as flags, but they also grew in colorful profusion in the gardens. As summer came on there were the dahlias, and in the dry summer there were zinnias and asters. Every back fence had a row of hollyhocks.

Those who had ample water grew roses. The soil and the climate were excellent and the pests were few in those days. The flowers were cut at the appropriate season and brought into the house to decorate the table and the living room. They were the pride of the country homemakers who found time from chores and endless responsibilities with families to grow the most wonderful flowers.

My mother taught me that if a person could afford two loaves of bread, he should buy one loaf and a lotus blossom. Edwin Markham, himself a rural western poet, wrote, "Three things a man must have if his soul would live and know life's perfect good. Three would the all supplying Father give; bread, beauty and brotherhood."

These were the words of the Ranchland.

CHAPTER 43

Photographs

Cameras hit the Ranchland early in the century. My first experience was with a box Brownie. It was very nearly foolproof and it took fairly good pictures. I cherished it as if it were a treasure from some mystic land.

Every camera was called a Kodak no matter what manufacturer had assembled a piece of equipment that could utilize film and preserve an image. I used my "Kodak" for special days when the family gathered and lined up on the front porch. I still have some faded copies of my early efforts. Those snapshots bring back memories of grandparents long gone and older relatives who are no more.

I once asked my parents how our ancestors preserved the images of days past. They explained to me that paintings of gatherings were much more common at earlier times, and that portraits were considered necessary in any family. I noticed that each ranch house had its share of family portraits hanging on the parlor walls. I soon discovered that tintypes were in use long before our handy little cameras were developed.

By the time I was in my teens I had a camera with a bellows that would slide out and make a much better image. It had a little trigger cord which disappeared under a dark sheet before snapping the shutter. I was then able to take better photos, but the fancy new cameras were much more trouble.

I had left the Ranchland before the days of light meters for each amateur. Our cameras, however, came in various sizes and used many different film sizes. Enlargements were known but not common; we simply used a larger camera with larger film to increase the size. We mailed our exposed films to Denver to get them developed. Sometimes it required a week or more to get the prints. Often we found we had made some mistake and the prints were blurred or worthless. Anyway, we had fun!

Only in my college days did I begin to use slides. Color was a great new addition to amateur photography. The color slides opened up a whole new world. Instead of the old gas lit stereopticons that could show us life in the far away places, we could visit our traveling neighbors and hear long and boring descriptions of "my trip."

I was once amused by a cartoon of the host darkening the room to show slides of some common sights while giving windy and boring descriptions. A guest couple was preparing to sneak out of the open window as soon as the show started!

Ranchers of today have camcorders for movies and zoom lenses for stills. Some have their own darkrooms for developing. Some instant cameras require no development. The old days were fun, but the new days are better! Three cheers for progress!

CHAPTER 44

The Mission of Medicine

Talk about national shortages. One of the greatest needs of the people of America, especially of us old people, is a new wave of recruits for general practice medicine. Specialists we have, probably the best in the world, but there is an alarming lack of young people who are willing and planning to enter the fields of family practice, geriatrics and primary care in general.

Where now are the dedicated medicos who brought babies into the world, diagnosed our needs, referred us to specialists, counseled us with regard to medical treatment and worked with us to live long lives of quality and meaning? Thank God for the few, but they are thinning out and the replacements are not in the medical schools.

In the Ranchland where I grew to manhood, I survived the deadly influenza, the measles, a murmuring heart, typhoid fever, and other life threatening illness with the help of a great Dr. Denny who covered a range of 20 miles with a team and buggy to keep us well and alive as long as possible. Today, in many places, a call for medical help may provide an opportunity to go several miles to an office on some future occasion when the doctor can find a free moment. Our only hope is in the emergency rooms of hospitals.

I am not unrealistic enough to ask for the golden days of house calls. All I ask is the availability of a learned physician who can relieve our illness and help us to live lives worth living. We have miracle drugs that can kill or cure; how are we to know when and which?

Why do medical students head for specialties? That is where the money is! *Forbes* magazine tells of a surgeon, Denton Cooley, whose income is $3,600,000! Our grandson, David Boyer, tells me that one of his classmates has entered the field of eye surgery and now has an annual income of $600,000 to $800,000. Many prominent physicians in specialties earn annual salaries approaching $500,000. With hopes of bonanzas like that, why should they fool around with the poor, the old and the ill who need primary care? The answer is that they need to give their lives to a noble cause. They are to be the new medical missionaries.

In 1950 I visited Nazareth in the then-new nation of Israel. My host was a physician who cared for the Arabs who populated the village. He presided at the hospital and was the one hope of the ailing. I asked him which church sent him there. He said, "Not a church; it was the Medical College of the University of Edinburgh." Money is not the only lure for those who would study medicine.

Do I know the cost of entering the field? Indeed I do. My own son is a distinguished medical professor. I hold we would do well to provide some scholarships for those who would do primary care for at least a decade after internship and boards. Call it impractical? I call it sensible and feasible.

America has the best medical care in the world and, in some cases, among the worst of the developed countries. We spend the most, but not always wisely. Socialized medicine? No. Support for some dedicated practitioners? Yes. A new contagion of missionary zeal? God help us to see the day!

CHAPTER 45

Denver

Denver was a clean and beautiful city. The air was pure and the mountains were a jagged skyline of majesty. The Denham Theater was equal to anything on Broadway. It was there I saw George Arliss play "Dinner At Eight." I knew he was a great artist, but I had not read *Up The Years From Bloomsbury*. When I learned of his fame I was proud to have seen him in person. I later enjoyed his "Disraeli," but that was on film. After rolling years of attending the theater in New York and London, I have seen no greater actor nor a more exciting play. My parents had treated me to true greatness when I was but a teenage ranch boy, and Denver had provided the theater.

With the coming of the automobile, Denver was only an hour away from our ranch. I was born with crooked teeth, and my parents drove me to Denver for an attempted correction. A jovial dentist named J. M. Norman did the best he could. At least I still have the teeth! The Denver visits were occasions for what we now call the stage and the cinema. One of the new actresses at The Denham was Gladys George. She went on to Broadway and London before she became famous in the movies.

I learned about department stores at Daniels and Fishers, the tallest building in Denver. I learned about the golden domed Capitol Building when Dad went to the office of Governor Shoup. I became familiar with many varieties of cars by visiting the showrooms; but of most interest to me were the displays of saddlery at Herman Henry Heiser's shop on Larimer Street. Saddles, chaps, boots, lariats, saddle blankets, scabbards, and other western gear held my attention for hours at a time. It was there I bought the tack that made me appear to be a cowboy.

My daydream then was to be a rancher with vast acres and many cattle. I dreamed of owning a few thousand acres in northern New Mexico where the landscape was wide and the sky was high but the land was cheap. One of my father's friends had a ranch there, which he had bought for $3 an acre. Land was $10 and over around our place and going up in price. Dreams change!

CHAPTER 46

College Days

A man named James E. Davis had started a small Bible college. He and our clergyman, W.A. Luce, conspired to enlist me in their new academic venture. While I was out in the field working in the hay, I saw a large black Buick drive up. Dr. James E. Davis, president of Colorado Bible College and pastor of the large Central Christian Church in Denver, stepped out and told me he had come personally to invite me to be a student at his college. I told him that I was a high school drop-out. He said, "We shall enroll you in night school at Denver Junior College, which is right across the street from our college, and there you can finish your high school work." With a sense of guilt for having dropped out of school, and a sense of interest in learning, I decided to go, even though I was afraid he would try to press me into the ministry, which I strongly resisted.

I drove my red Buick to Denver, found

lodging, and began the course of study. It was a fine little college. The high school tutoring at Denver Junior College was much to my liking. I breezed through elementary chemistry, geography, mathematics and literature. Within a year or two, I had completed the course and had won my high school diploma.

With regard to the fear that I would be pressed into the ministry, I found that it had been truly justified. Within a year, Dr. Davis had sent me out to preach at Cherry Creek Grange, where a small Sunday school and church had been developed. This was near Franktown. I worked hard on my sermon. The harder I worked the more confused I came to be. I had been told I should have three points and a text. My text was to be, "And God said, let there be light." I hammered out three points: the darkness, the command, and the light. Logical enough, but how to fill it out and make it relevant? I worked it out to the best of my ability and, with considerable anxiety, awaited Sunday morning

Come Sunday morning I was up early. I breakfasted on cereal, which was my usual way, to save money. I hopped into my red Buick and took off for Cherry Creek, about 20 miles away.

The weather was as clear as the day of Creation must have been. I was dressed in a navy suit and wore a stiff collar with buttons. I held my head up very straight to avoid discomfort.

The road along Cherry Creek was fairly level, and I breezed along at about 45 miles an hour, fast for those days. A few chickens scattered as I came along. One rooster took wing, and before I could stop I heard a slight bump. I pulled to a stop and looked around. There was no sign that I had hit him. I proceeded on, thinking that the rooster had made it home safe and unbruised. Before I expected, I arrived at the Grange Hall.

I was early for church. A few men were gathered outside the building, talking about farming affairs, no doubt, when one of them came over to my car as I was getting out. He reached over one fender and, from between the hood and the fender, he grabbed the rooster and held it up — dead — as if the execution had been planned.

The valley re-echoed with their laughter. One man said, "Preacher, you are the first parson I ever heard of that brought his chicken dinner with him!"

I was embarrassed. My efforts to explain were laughed down. One of the men agreed to take the bird home for Sunday dinner.

I went on into the hall to see what could be done. The superintendent of the Sunday school presided at the service and led the singing. I sat nervously through the proceedings until he introduced me by telling the rooster tale.

I arose to preach. I plunged into the sermon with strong voice and some fire. I quoted the text, hammered home the three points, gave the conclusion and glanced at my large pocket watch. Less than five minutes had elapsed. I knew that the congregation would know I was a greenhorn and feel cheated for having asked me to

come. I had prepared a second sermon for the
evening, so I launched into it. I was able to fill in
another five minutes. This was the end. I
announced that the evening service had been
canceled, said the benediction and headed for
Denver.

Since then I have preached in some of the
greatest churches of Christendom, but have never
felt quite at home in the role of a clergyman. My
neighbor and colleague in Detroit, Herbert
Hudnut, spoke the truth when he observed,
"Perry, the cloth is too tight on you." He was
right. I went on to teach and to become "The Old
Professor."

CHAPTER 47

Early Business Interest

My years in Denver were few, but very significant. It was there that I developed my three great interests, one of which has been my life. One was business, another was developing churches, and the third, which controls my destiny, was teaching. When I was ordained into the ministry, as was the custom in that Bible College, I was ordained to teach. I have followed that compelling gleam throughout my long life.

When I was living at home on the ranch, I had developed something of the art of business. I knew, almost instinctively, that the art consisted of buying low and selling high. I also learned the importance of frugality. I was never one to spend money recklessly and, as time went on, I learned the true secret of every business, which is the sandbag on sales and the broad axe on expenses. I inherited a portion of the family ranch, and I held it until my early 80s. I deeded it over to my son with the hope that a portion of that old ranch would stay in the family.

I caught my interest in developing churches from Dr. Davis, President of the Bible College, and the other members of the faculty. The teacher who meant the most to me taught me the Greek language. His name was Allen Miller. He went from there to a great career in academics, having earned a Ph.D. in his biblical studies. He became Episcopal Bishop of Easton, Maryland. In that capacity he was chaplain to Presidents Truman, Eisenhower and Roosevelt. At this writing he is 90 years old and is one of my most cherished friends still. He lives in Naples, Florida.

With the encouragement of my colleagues in the Bible College, I took over a tiny congregation meeting in a basement located near the University of Denver. I was very successful in developing that congregation. We soon had enough members and enough pledges to begin building a superstructure. We called it the Bungalow Church, for the building was made for a home when and if its church days were accomplished. A little at a time, I enlisted free labor from the carpenters, bricklayers and cement people of the neighborhood. I wheedled the material from the lumber yards, the brick yards and the hardware companies. Within a year we had begun to build, and within two years it was completed. I worked hand-in-hand with each of the workmen, except those who had such technical skill as was required in laying brick or pouring cement.

The interesting fact is that practically all

those who worked on the building became members of the congregation. On the day we dedicated, my old friends from the choir of Central Christian Church came out to sing. Those wonderful men not only sang, but they gave several thousand dollars toward paying for the furnishings for the building. It was an exciting story in *The Denver Post.*

CHAPTER 48

Courtship and Marriage

I have mentioned the three predominant
interests that developed in my Denver days, but I
have not yet mentioned my overriding and
overwhelming interest in a beautiful young
soprano named Elsie Stanbrough. We met as we
both sang in the choir of Central Christian
Church, then located on Lincoln Street. She had
a modest voice with a wide range. There was a
sweet quality to her singing which enchanted
everybody, especially me. I asked to drive her
home from choir practice and she accepted.

We made excursions up into the mountains,
played tennis, visited the amusement park and
enjoyed working with the little congregation that
met in the basement. The air was crystal clear
then, and our hearts were young and vibrant. We
fell deeply in love.

I, with a practical turn of mind, said, "When
I finish my education and am located as a teacher,

we should marry." She would have none of it.
With the unerring instinct of a bright woman who
was already serving as private secretary to the
local president of Conoco Oil Company, she said,
"No, it is now or never." As nearly always
happens, we compromised and were married! It
was a simple ceremony in the basement church.
John Scott said the marriage vows, in as much as
Allen Miller and Dr. Davis were both out of town.
One of Billy Sunday's great trombonists and
soloists was a friend of ours and came out to sing.
Church members and friends, as well as family,
swarmed the building. We were as happy as two
young mountain goats. The choir of Central
Christian Church devoted a large fellowship
dinner in our honor and showered us with
wedding gifts.

Elsie's parents and their friends were
skeptical about Elsie's marriage to a young ranch
lad who had not yet found gainful employment
beyond the small salary paid to him by the tiny
church, but Elsie was persuasive and they all
joined in the celebration.

My red Buick had worn out and had been
sold. When the wedding was over, my father and
mother presented me with the keys to a new Ford.

CHAPTER 49

The Lure of Texas

The Bible College fell into hard times when Dr. Davis retired and entered the ice cream business in Indiana. Some members of the faculty moved the college to Fort Collins and joined in with what was then the Colorado Agricultural College. For a year I was in attendance, but the arrangement was not very satisfactory. Elsie and I returned to Denver; she to her secretarial work and I to my little bungalow church.

The new pastor of Central Christian Church was a solid Texan named Paul G. Preston. He took me under his wing at once and arranged for Elsie and me to move to Texas, where I could study at Texas Christian University. This allowed me to develop my dream of being a university professor. And after several years of dedicated study, this dream came true. It was there I began to teach in 1933.

The goodbyes to Denver were difficult because we loved many people and were loved by them in return; but, the most difficult goodbye was out at the ranch when my aging parents said their last farewell as we drove off toward Texas. It was a tearful occasion. They knew instinctively that my ranch days were over. And while I have continued my interest in the ranch and ownership of a remainder of it, the thought of returning to ranching has not occurred to me.

CHAPTER 50

The Lure of the Ranchland

In June of 1992 I returned to my Ranchland home. We gathered at the Elbert Christian Church where I attended as a boy, and then proceeded to the Strickland Tea Room for a family brunch. Time has taken its toll, but there was a goodly number. The young keep coming to replace the old who are heading for the last roundup. It seems strange to realize that I am now the older generation. George and Mary Gresham are long gone. Only Harvey, Bernice and I are still around.

No sensitive person who has ever felt the bite of the northwest wind, known the exhilaration of Indian paintbrush on the hills of spring, heard the sound of the meadow lark on a pasture fence post or felt the vibrancy of a good saddle horse beneath him can ever forget. This was my home, and I returned to it as naturally as the salmon brave the steep rocks of the Columbia River to spawn.

I can never forget the drive through the Black Forest on the way past Table Rock to the village of Elbert which nestles into the jack pines hard by the meandering Kiowa Creek. Nor the drive from Castle Rock which traverses the piney road past Elizabeth and Kiowa on the way to Elbert. As I passed the cemetery I remembered the three generations of Greshams and Eplers who are sleeping there. We had buried my brother, Daniel Franklin, there in December of 1990. When I stopped to read the other dear names, I found friends of my youth who were leaders of that Divide Country when I was a stripling.

Again I saw such familiar names as Calhan, Simla, Fondis, Peyton, Limon, Agate, Falcon, and all the places that were household words as I grew toward manhood. This was a sentimental journey to my land of home.

As my plane flew over those familiar hills and prairies, I craned my neck to see if I could still identify any of the hills, gullies, creeks and pine fringed canyons that were my haunts. Pikes Peak, Devil's Head, Mt. Evans and Longs Peak fascinated me once again. That western horizon is for me the land of "Over the hills and far away."

The old gang is decimated, if not gone, but I have new friends, and I am young and vital once again! The lure of the Ranchland is forever!

CHAPTER 51

Ranchland Revisited

June in the Ranchland is a time to remember. We drove eastward from Colorado Springs on the way to Elbert. Along the way we saw a small herd of pronghorn antelope moving silently along as if there were no human predators anywhere in the world. I marvel that they go under fences as limbo dancers go beneath the barriers.

The day was bright and sunny. The air was clean and clear as if filtered through a gathering of snow white cumulus clouds. When we turned left at Peyton we were alone on the road. The pavement was quite different than the ruts and gravel I once knew. We pulled into Elbert to find it smaller than when I moved away 78 years ago. The railroad was gone. The Roman Catholic Church had closed its doors. The Russell Gates Mercantile Company was a community hall. The bank was a funny little shell of a building long uninhabited. Many of my familiar haunts had been swept away in the flood of 1936.

The Presbyterian Church still commanded the center of the village from its perch on the hillside. We drove on east past the new school building, which is no longer new, to the cemetery on the top of a hill. There the pioneers of the Greshams and the Eplers have found a final place to rest. God knows they needed it, for the dates on the stones go back to the late 1800s. Ranch life was, and is, hard work.

We returned to the Christian Church where I was the guest speaker. I had joined that congregation in 1919. Only a few veterans survived, but those of us who were still around enjoyed a jolly reunion. We are all a bit wrinkled and beat up, but we have spirit or we would not be here! Lila Tyler, Henry Carnahan and I are part of the diminishing remnant.

After church we convened at the Elbert tea room for a family brunch. There were 45 Greshams and Eplers on hand! We made the Monty Gaddys and the Ken Hoschouers honorary members.

The storm clouds were organizing as we drove out to the old Gresham ranch house. Just as we arrived a thunderstorm struck. The wind blew so hard it took two men to hold one man's hair on! The lightning flashed and the thunder roared, but we were inside and the rain soon passed. The house seemed smaller than the one we built in 1912! Actually, it is larger, for Danny and Kim, who now own it, have added space.

The James Seeleys, our niece and nephew, drove us back to Colorado Springs. We said good night to Howard and Bernice Roberts, my sister and her husband; then we drove back to our hotel with wonderful memories.

CHAPTER 52

The Groves of Academe

The Ranchland led me to Denver where I received a wife, a dream and an appetite for learning. I drove our Pontiac sedan along graveled roads toward Fort Worth, Texas; more accurately, toward Texas Christian University, where I was to begin a life in higher education. I crammed college into three years and began the joint venture of student instructor and graduate student. I loved learning and, to this day, I am still a student. I started teaching at age 24, and it has been my life.

I found a vast new world at the University of Chicago. There I met Ames in philosophy, Knight in economics and Garrison in history. I was enchanted with these great teachers whose books I had read. Ames, Garrison and T.V. Smith became my friends for life. I returned to T.C.U. determined to pursue a life of scholarship.

President E.M. Waits, who was about to

retire, and some of the trustees, as well as a few of my faculty colleagues, mentioned me as a likely successor to Dr. Waits. I knew the possibility was remote, but I took a leave of absence from teaching philosophy to study university administration at Columbia University in New York. While I was away an older and more experienced president was chosen. When I returned to T.C.U. my life was a bit uncomfortable. When an attractive opportunity came, I left my friends in Fort Worth and my cherished colleagues at T.C.U. and drove to Seattle, Washington. By then we were three. Our wonderful son, Glen, had come to center stage in our lives. He was coming on ten years of age.

The University of Washington, where I lectured, and the University Christian Church, where I preached, consumed every moment of our lives. After five years, however, I was off for Detroit, Michigan, where a similar church and university relationship invited me. I lectured at The University of Michigan in Ann Arbor and preached at the famous old Central Woodward Church in Detroit. While there, my beautiful young wife, Elsie, died from a sudden thrombosis. Glen and I lived on, lonely, but mutually sustaining one another. Glen finished high school and went on to Harvard College. At the time of his graduation, I was invited to become president of Bethany College in West Virginia.

Glen and I spent our summers abroad. He conducted tours, and I lectured and wrote for the Detroit Free Press. While I was in Beirut, he lived